For the Love of
TRUTH

A Rational Approach to Belief in a Creator

REV. JACK DAVENPORT

GROUND TRUTH PRESS
BOX ELDER, SOUTH DAKOTA

For the Love of Truth:

A Rational Approach to Belief in a Creator

Copyright © 2023 Rev. Jack Davenport

Published by

GROUND TRUTH PRESS
514 Americas Way, PMB 19000
Box Elder, SD 57719

Copy Editor: Bonnie Lyn Smith
Cover Design: Bonnie Lyn Smith

Cover Photo Credits:
shutterstock.com/JuShoot/1897649500
Image(s) used under license from Shutterstock.com

Interior Photo Credits:
Double beaver dam: FreeImages.com/zulu
DNA-structure-and-bases: Wikimedia Commons/File:DNA-structure-and-bases.png

Names:	Davenport, Jack, 1953- author.
Title:	For the love of truth : a rational approach to belief in a Creator / Rev. Jack Davenport.
Description:	Box Elder, South Dakota : Ground Truth Press, [2024] | Includes bibliographical references.
Identifiers:	ISBN: 979-89870508-5-9 (paperback) | LCCN: 2024906358
Subjects:	LCSH: Truth--Religious aspects--Christianity. | Holiness. | Faith. | Christian life. | Apologetics. | Religion and science. | BISAC: RELIGION / Christian Theology / Apologetics. | RELIGION / Religion & Science. | PHILOSOPHY / Epistemology.
Classification:	LCC: BT50 .D38 2024 | DDC: 230.01--dc23

First printing 2024
Printed in the United States of America

Trade paperback ISBN-13: 979-8-9870508-5-9

To my friend, Schmoul,
who now knows the truth he spent his life seeking

Table of Contents

PREFACE

I didn't set out to write this book. I'd been writing monthly articles for my church newsletter and had just completed one entitled "Desire Holiness." My sister appreciated the *head knowledge* in the article but was left wondering how, having the desire for holiness, she might fulfill God's call in *practice*: "As [God] who called you is holy, you also be holy in all your conduct" (*English Standard Version Bible*, 2016, 1 Pet. 1:15). She asked me to follow the initial article with another one offering advice for reaching, or at least actively pursuing, that goal. Well, I'm not all that practically minded, and I knew her request would be quite a challenge, but it made sense to try to follow the article about *right desire* with *realistic guidance* for living in this world.

Like many of life's pursuits, if you don't know what the goal is, you won't know whether you reach it. In fact, you won't even know where to aim. As an example, I like to play golf. One of the tips for improved results is to picture in your mind the shot you are about to make. Why? Because you'll most often swing the club (and hit the ball) the way you've pictured, whether you've envisioned the ball going into the water or landing on the green.

Likewise, my article on desiring holiness had assumed that every reader had a similar (and accurate) understanding of the ultimate goal—holiness—or would come to that awareness without much help. But apparently that wasn't the case. I couldn't talk about practical steps *to* holiness when there were almost as many opinions *about* holiness as there were people. Some people would have been focused on the pitfalls to holiness just like the golfer who can't keep his mind off the water, while others would have ignored any discussion of it, believing they had already achieved some measure of holiness. So, as I began to write the article on practical holiness, I could see that I needed to address many views about holiness to bring us all to a common understanding; and that led me to explore the foundation upon which these views were built—an understanding of truth.

In short, I'd begun writing an article in which I'd assumed that the reader had a basic belief in Jesus Christ as Savior. To my surprise, it developed into a book that plumbs the depth of biblical truth, the foundation of holiness. Returning to my golf analogy, once I could envision a perfect swing, it became clear how the flaws in my swing were causing the bad shots I wanted to avoid. Until we truly understand how to carry out a task or achieve a goal, we tend to assume that our initial perceptions are correct. The only way to test our perceptions is to return to the basics, beginning anew with uncomplicated ideas that we can understand and agree on.

In the same way, I began to search for any elemental truths about holiness that would provide the building blocks for discussing the steps to holiness. As I proceeded along this path, however, I found that I was challenging many preconceived notions within popular Christian culture—some that came from parents, school, or church, and some that came from society at large. I couldn't expose the flaws in those ideas without dealing with the more significant questions of biblical truth: what truth is and how we come to know it. The more I wrote, the more issues I discovered. I couldn't draw the article to a close, and I found myself addressing a wider audience than I had first envisioned. What began as a study of holiness became an examination of right thinking and the truth that leads to faith, which are the foundation of holiness. And it dawned on me that I had the makings of a book.

I pray that you find reading this book as enjoyable and thought-provoking as I have found writing it. And I hope even more that whatever your current spiritual state, you will come to know, love, and follow the truth of Jesus more deeply.

Note to the Reader:

Some of the material in this book assumes specific knowledge that the reader may not have. The appendices explore a few concepts in greater depth as a resource to supplement the main text of the book. Refer to the appendices for helpful background information.

1
A Search for Truth

The Love of Wisdom

So, how do we gain understanding? How do we know when we have
found truth?

It is the work of philosophy to study and find truth. The average
person, however, often looks upon the work of philosophy with
skepticism or even disapproval, as the occupation of those who idly
speculate about ideas that have no value for those of us living in the
real world. The Apostle Paul warns us, saying, "See to it that no one
takes you captive by philosophy and empty deceit, according to
human tradition, according to the elemental spirits of the world"
(Col. 2:8). But notice that Paul does not tell anyone to avoid
philosophy. His warning is to avoid *becoming a prisoner (even a slave)* to
those philosophies of the world that are based on false ideas. Paul,
himself, uses philosophical techniques to attack false reasoning and
promote right thinking in his writings.

Philosophy per se is not the problem. After all, "philosophy"
means "love of wisdom." As the book of Proverbs declares, "The
beginning of wisdom is this: Get wisdom, and whatever you get, get
insight. Prize her highly, and she will exalt you; she will honor you if
you embrace her" (Prov. 4:7-8). But not all philosophy is good.
Faulty reasoning leads to bad philosophy, to a way of thinking and

acting that is not consistent with the truth. New ideas generally don't take root immediately, but they will, like yeast, work their way through the culture over the course of time before anyone has thought deeply about them, taking captive those who are unaware.[1]

For instance, by the late 20th century, the philosophy of postmodernism was challenging modernism as the commonly accepted foundation for reasoning in our culture.[2] The modernist believed that there were objective truths about this world that were established through observation and reason and were true for all people, regardless of the time or culture in which they lived.[3] Postmodernists, on the other hand, questioned the objective, universal nature of truth, suggesting that truth claims were unquestionably true only for the person making them, as in, true *for thee* but not *for me*.[4] So, if you were born toward the end of the 20th century, it is likely that you were exposed to and absorbed some postmodern ways of understanding this world and truth, even if you have never heard of postmodernism.

Is either philosophy—modernism or postmodernism—right? Is there a better, even a *best*, philosophy? Any way of thinking that obscures the truth or lays claim to greater wisdom than we have reason to profess is "bad" philosophy. Taking Paul seriously, we want to avoid becoming a prisoner of those wrong ideas that can easily invade our thought life and hold us hostage. By contrast, the love of wisdom yields good philosophy, which can set people free from false ideas. I wrote this book for love of the truth, and I invite the reader along with me as we seek the truth together.

During His interrogation by Pontius Pilate, Jesus said, "Everyone who is of the truth listens to my voice" (John 18:37). Many of you may recognize Pilate's infamous reply, "What is truth?" (John 18:38). The question demands an answer, yet the one that the Gospel of John provides can only be understood after a thorough examination and unraveling of the confusion that confounds the search for truth. This is not a book that assumes the Bible to be true.

My purpose is to lead the reader on a journey to find truth, to challenge error and misconceptions, and to provide the reader with a foundation for walking in the light of truth.

The Truth About Reality

But how do we come to know truth? According to the *Merriam-Webster Dictionary*, truth may be defined as:[5]

1. "the body of true statements and propositions"
2. "the property (as of a statement) of being in accord with fact or reality"

The first instance defines truth as a collection of all things that are true, while the second is about the essence of truth. The former raises the question whether we need to know all possible true statements and propositions about reality before we can claim to know the truth. The latter suggests that truth can be known to the extent that we grasp the fundamental nature of this world. In either case, it seems we need to know something about reality to have access to truth.

The concepts of truth and reality are so closely linked that it can be difficult to talk about one without considering or confusing it with the other. They are different, yet bound together, like two sides of a coin. Any statement of truth assumes that the speaker's view of reality is correct...including this one, and any particular depiction of reality can lead us to wonder whether and in what way it is true. In the remainder of this chapter we will look closely at reality to see whether there is anything that we can accept with confidence about it and, if so, what that might be.

Perhaps we should start by asking what we mean by the word *reality*. The *Merriam-Webster Dictionary* online gives the following definitions:[6]

1. the quality or state of being real
2. a real event, entity, or state of affairs

3. the totality of real things and events

4. something that is neither derivative nor dependent but exists necessarily

The problem with that dictionary definition, however, is what it boils down to: "reality is the collection of all that is real." But that doesn't clarify anything, does it? It's not easy to talk about reality without falling into the trap of using terms that are grounded in our concepts of reality in order to describe it.

I used to have a red car ("merlot" according to the manufacturer). Sodium street and parking lot lights have a funny effect on red cars, though; under that lighting my car turned a mysterious bluish-gray. Upon leaving work the first night after my company had moved offices to a new location, I had difficulty finding my car in the lot. I saw a car that had the right shape and size and was in the same area I had parked during the day, but I could not convince myself that it was my car until I checked the license plate and realized that the lighting had changed my car's appearance.

I would see red when my car was sitting in sunlight, but under sodium street lighting, my car seemed to change color. Was my car *actually* red, or not? It wasn't simply that my car would gradually disappear from sight as daylight faded. We need light reflecting from real objects to be able to see them, and the lighting in the parking lot was sufficient for me to see. But if the physical makeup of my car did not change when its color changed, I had to wonder whether red was the *real* color of my car. If its real color depended on the reflected light, then was the color I could see in daylight real? The answer depends on one's perspective.

Let's consider another example: whether it could be that our eyes are playing tricks on us. We know that some people see the same scenes differently. While some people have difficulty distinguishing certain colors and are said to be colorblind, and others have an additional set of eye cones (the color receptors of the eye) that give them exceptional color vision,[7] most of us have so-called "normal" vision. Yet even people with normal vision sometimes see colors differently from others.

It may be that the person with an acute ability to discern shades of color would identify my car's color as "merlot," not just "red," but that has to do with their ability to detect nuances of color, not the reality of the color of my car. Think of it this way: Even those of us who have difficulty correctly describing the colors of a landscape could still distinguish a poor artistic representation of that scene from a good one. In fact, we would immediately recognize a painting as true-to-life if it accurately portrayed a landscape—a kind of "That's it!" moment.

Despite our various capabilities, in daylight we could be reasonably certain that all but those who were colorblind would see that my car was some kind of red. The color wouldn't change with the person who was viewing it, nor would its color only be a matter of personal preference or opinion. So, we can infer that my car appeared to have an odd color under sodium lighting because its yellow light wouldn't reflect as red light, even from a red car. It was the lighting that had changed—not my car. People would perceive my car as red, not because they imagined or dreamed it, but because it *really* was red.

All the evidence suggests that for most people, the world we *think* we live in is, in fact, the world we *actually* live in, not the product of our personal imaginations or dreams. Still, could it be that our experiences in this world are not real but, rather, illusions or the result of some kind of mind game?

No, while optical illusions fool our mind's eye so that what we think we see is different from what's actually there, optical illusions are not visual experiences that are beyond our understanding. Quite the contrary, it is well understood that our minds can interpret certain information apart from the physical reality of what is being observed.[8] How do we know that? We can usually measure or test what we see with instruments that clarify the physical reality even though our eyes may fool us, such as with the common example below, in which the two sets of horizontal lines are actually the same length:

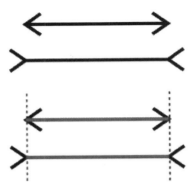

Remember the image of "*The dress*" that was on the internet, where some people saw the dress as gold and white and others as black and blue?[9] No one thought that the disagreeing observers were living in wholly different realities; people knew it had to be an optical illusion. Most of the time, we can trust what we see, but even when we're fooled by an optical illusion, we have the tools to confirm the correct way of understanding the illusion so that we can ultimately determine what is real.

We know how to deal with illusions that fool our eyes, but what about our minds? Maybe the world we experience keeps us from knowing the world as it really is, similar to the premise of the movie *The Truman Show*, where the main character (Truman Burbank) doesn't initially realize that what he thinks is his real life is actually a scripted TV show?[10] Truman eventually determines that there are serious problems with the reality he is experiencing as inconsistencies and impossibilities begin to register in his mind. By the end of the movie, he rejects the reality that he had been raised to believe was normal, and he learns about the true reality that created his learned— but false—world. The movie illustrates that our reality is at least partially dependent on what our minds accept as true.

We can measure and test physical realities to know how the world actually works, but there is a psychological dimension of reality that cannot be so easily confined to scientific and logical argumentation. It is possible for the mind to be deceived, but that is not because the physical reality we live in is false. If we misperceive, make false assumptions, or have false beliefs about reality, then *the reality we live by* will be false, just as it was for Truman until he discerned the truth and came to know reality as it actually was.

Despite our physical limitations, illusions that trick our minds, or outright attempts to deceive us, it seems we do have (or can establish) an accurate picture of the world as it actually is, that is, of reality.

Reality in Context

No matter who we are, we have limited ability to experience and investigate the world in which we live. As a result, our ideas about reality are restricted to our direct experiences by virtue of the five senses, what we have learned or read from others, and what we have come to know on our own through careful examination and reflection. Our view of reality is also dependent on the setting or context in which we attempt to understand this world, just as the appearance of my car depended on the light reflecting from it.

Think about the images on our TV or computer screens. What we see as a picture is, in fact, a collection of thousands of little red, green and blue dots (called "pixels") that the human brain is able to stitch together into a complete image. The ordering, shading and coloring of the dots are determined by the picture that is to be formed. Apart from the dots there is no picture, and apart from the picture there is no purpose for the dots. Both are real but are understood from different perspectives or in distinct contexts. By contrast, paint spattered on a piece of paper might occasionally form a shape that looks like a known image or object, but it would be virtually impossible for a random paint spatter to accurately and completely depict some aspect of reality. For instance, we sometimes see cloud formations that remind us of a familiar animal, but those "images" are really only random shapes. If we say, "That cloud looks like a lamb," we don't mean that the cloud's purpose is to display the image of a lamb or that the idea of a lamb had some control over how the cloud was formed. Cloud formations are real, but any resemblance to people, creatures, or things is purely accidental.

The study of reality in differing contexts often leads to an expanded understanding and even a corrected assessment of the way the world actually is, demonstrating that what is real is not strictly limited to that which we can perceive with the five senses or even what can be accessed with the aid of modern technology. For instance, we can't "see" the electricity in our homes, but we know it's "there" by the lights and appliances it powers. Even when technicians or scientists work with electricity, they can't actually see the moving electrons that produce the effect we call "electricity." While we may not know much about electrons, most of us are glad that electricity plays an important role in our reality.

Comprehending All Reality

Because we as humans don't have direct access to *the whole* of reality, we sometimes hear about experts changing their views on some aspect of their field of study. New medical "truths" seem to emerge almost weekly, often reversing what was previously thought to be true. And what is a discovery but the uncovering of a certain aspect of reality that was previously unknown, such as a new kind of plant or animal or a new comet or galaxy? Even people who dedicate their lives to better understanding a specific, narrow feature of the world do not have perfect knowledge of their own field, much less all of reality.

Accordingly, if researchers who pursue lifelong fields of study are not immune to a mistaken or incomplete understanding of reality—even within their specialty—then the rest of us must also have misconceptions and imperfect knowledge. Sometimes people make statements of "fact" in daily conversation only to have someone with greater knowledge of that subject matter point out an error in their understanding. No one has a handle on the full extent of reality. The entire collection of human knowledge barely scratches the surface of all there is to know.

Not only that, but many of the ideas we take for granted as facts are actually beliefs—concepts we have come to rely upon but can never know to be true with absolute certainty. For instance, we take for granted the principles we call "Natural Laws," and we believe they accurately describe reality because scientists have used them innumerable times and have found that they provide correct results. Thus, we conclude—in that we *believe* or *trust*—that they will produce accurate results the next time they are employed as well. Until we fully grasp the notion that we **all** live by faith when it comes to some of our "knowledge" of reality, we are vulnerable to believing ideas about reality that are simply false.

Some people may think it is simply a matter of time before we get our arms around the whole of reality, that every day we come closer to that goal as scientists unravel the mysteries of the universe. But does the evidence—or reason—support such a claim? Prior to the advent of the telescope, those who studied the night sky named individual stars and constellations, understanding that some constellations could be seen only at certain times of year. Those early astronomers studied the few "stars" that appeared to move against the background of the constellations and called them "wanderers," from a Greek word that we translate as "planets." With the invention of the telescope, astronomers saw that the planets were of a different makeup than the stars and that some of the lights that appeared to be stars were, instead, clusters of many, many stars—what we now call "galaxies." As we developed more powerful telescopes and new instruments to study the universe, scientists have been able to see into some of the deepest recesses of space. Our knowledge of the world beyond Earth has grown—and continues to grow—exponentially.

What about the study of our own planet and of life itself? From the structure of the living cell to the forces that drive our weather and other natural phenomena, we have gained amazing knowledge. But has *what we now know* grown as fast as *what we still do not know*? Just as with the example from the discipline of astronomy, the more we have learned, the more we have uncovered to be studied. It seems that every new discovery or theory opens a door to even greater complexities that we have yet to research. Our collective experience suggests that we do not now, nor ever will, know or understand all that embodies the universe.

Someone Outside

Have you ever "unplugged" on vacation, only to return home feeling like you'd lost touch with the world? A major event might have occurred of which you were completely unaware, but the situation was already "old news." You were living in your own little world, not paying any attention to the news. But isn't that part of *why* you went on vacation in the first place—to "get away from it all"? In a sense, you created your own little reality apart from the greater whole. With no information flowing to you from the outside world, you were able to live as if your reality was all that mattered. This example will help us as we think about **universal reality**, that is, the way things *actually* are from the perspective of someone viewing the universe *from the outside*.

When we think of reality in terms of context, what we mean is understanding reality one aspect at a time, according to one's perspective. We attempt to observe portions of the world corresponding to our areas of interest as if we were outsiders looking in. That's why scientists are careful to set up experiments to minimize the likelihood that they themselves will influence the results, just as if they were truly able to observe the world from the outside-in. We certainly gain some understanding of reality in this manner, but what we learn is limited to the specific area of interest. Unfortunately, we never have the opportunity to step outside the universe and look at

all reality. In truth, we are not outsiders looking in on reality but, rather, insiders trying to understand the kind of "box" in which we are living.

Returning to our vacation scenario, suppose you travel to an isolated island having limited contact with the outside world, relaxing without a care when the power and phone lines suddenly go down. At first, you think the wind caused a tree to fall on some main lines. But nobody on the island knows what caused the outage, nor is anyone able to communicate with the mainland to find out. With the power and all phones out of service, everyone on the island is in the dark—literally and figuratively. You begin to speculate, just as scientists would. You develop your own theories and test them as best you can against the available evidence. "Could it have been a major earthquake?" "Maybe, but we didn't feel any shaking." "Suppose it was a power failure." "What about a terrorist attack?" The problem is that nobody has a way to determine which, if any, of your theories is correct until and unless someone *from outside the island* tells you what happened.

That is exactly the situation in which we find ourselves in this world. Unless "someone" is able to view the universe from outside it, to tell us the way the world *actually* is, we can never be sure we have an accurate and complete understanding of the whole of reality. We have the *impression* that we have a thorough understanding of much of the universe, but we are effectively restricted to clusters of knowledge. We are constrained by imperfect and limited senses, so much so that the most intelligent person would never be able to know or understand all there is to know about the universe. Even a group of scientists working together can observe only a small portion of the earth's processes during their lifetimes. What if we were to combine all the efforts of all people for all time? In a sense we do— or at least we try to—inasmuch as what we now know or have learned has its foundation in the efforts of those who have gone before us.[11] But we still fall woefully short of being able to grasp—let alone achieve—the knowledge of the whole of reality, despite having ready access to the world's knowledge through the internet. Although some of our theories about the whole of reality could be correct, we cannot know that for certain. We are constrained by the very reality we are trying to understand, just as in the vacation example.

Think of medicine, astronomy, law, and geography as pockets of knowledge, and the known facts within those fields of study as bits or pieces of knowledge. The experts put together pieces of knowledge to slowly develop their fields and try to identify and correct misconceptions. Every field of study has its gaps in understanding, a lack of sufficient pieces to create a complete picture, and even false ideas. Put simply, *we don't know what we don't know.* So, how do we define a universal reality when we can *never* have a complete picture of the universe by studying it from within?

CONSIDER THIS

How do we define a universal reality when we can *never* have a complete picture of the universe by studying it from within?

Worldview as a Framework

Our inability to comprehend universal reality "from outside" has significant implications. Lacking *definitive* knowledge of the universe's structure, we are left to establish our own universal framework within which to fit our constellations of knowledge. We call this framework our "**worldview**," those overarching principles that govern how we interpret reality.

So, for instance, someone might hold a view that reality is composed entirely of material things and that all existence, events, and actions (including the behaviors of living things) can be explained in terms of the laws governing nature, and human beings are evolved animals. The person with this view might hold that the universe came into being of its own accord by virtue of those natural laws, or has always been in existence. There is no room for a creator, at least not one who might be expected to supply the perspective of someone viewing the universe from outside. Consequently, knowledge of this world would be limited to the discoveries and theories of those inside, but they could never know with any confidence that their understanding of the whole of reality was correct or complete. Through such a worldview, it would be reasonable to conclude that there are no universal moral laws because there would be no ultimate (or universal) lawgiver; any common moral code would be whatever people generally agreed upon.

On the other hand, someone who believes a creator brought the physical world into existence would likely see in that creator a rational cause for nature and a foundation for reality apart from and having greater authority than the knowledge originating in human beings. For instance, a person's view of the creator's role in the formation of life would dramatically affect that person's understanding of the position and function of humanity. In the most explicitly developed form of this view, people are not animals but specially created moral beings bearing the characteristics of their creator and having responsibility for the care of the world in which they live. Consequently, their legal system would be grounded in a universal morality, a morality that comes from the creator. The laws by which the physical universe operates would be seen not as chance happenings but rather as signs of an intelligent creator imposing order on his creation to be discovered by his creatures. In this worldview, science would become the project of understanding in what ways the creator brought the world into being and sustains it. As a result, there would be no conflict between faith and science in this view because reality would encompass both.

Our worldview clearly affects the way in which we live, but how do we identify (or choose) our worldview? Needing to order the world in which we live, each of us naturally constructs a framework in our minds—a worldview. Day by day, we gather ideas about reality from what we observe, learn, and reason on our own, or sometimes we simply absorb the views of others (or our culture) without questioning whether those notions accurately describe reality. Since we are part of reality, observing it from within, we can never quite grasp how to properly piece together our personal bits of knowledge. The truth about reality is that it is something different from and greater than what any of us can fully comprehend. Consequently, we each develop (consciously or unconsciously) a personal understanding of reality within which we fit our notions of the way the world is. A correct and complete worldview can only be derived from a *perfect understanding* of the whole of reality. But since we can never put together a perfect picture of reality from within, we are all mistaken in some conception of it.

To the degree that we fail to understand and account for this, we run the risk of replacing the definition of reality with our own incomplete or even invalid worldview, interpreting our observations of the world to correspond to that worldview rather than redefining our worldview according to the way the world *actually* is. The problem is that our worldviews can become more real to us than reality itself, becoming the "lenses" through which we observe and further refine our understanding of reality. Our worldviews are essentially our "reality-views," our individual conceptions of reality. As a result, we often impose our incomplete and potentially false worldviews on reality instead of allowing reality to inform and correct our worldviews. To the degree that this is true for each of us, we are living a fantasy, a la Truman Burbank, acting as if our personal conception of reality is more real than reality itself.

The corrective is to understand and then live in the world as it *actually* is, not the way we would like it to be, to allow reality to form our worldviews. But how are we to fully live in this world *as it actually is* if our knowledge of this world is constrained to what we know from *within* the reality we are trying to understand? As we gain greater understanding of the world around us, we should constantly be asking whether our worldview needs adjusting to fit the true reality.

The Fullness of Reality

How do we get out of this predicament? How can we overcome the limitations imposed by our worldviews? The answer is to discover a worldview that makes sense of every aspect of reality, at least to the degree we can know it. Unfortunately, unless someone from outside our reality tells us what we are missing and misunderstanding about this world, we are limited to our own efforts at studying reality from within.

There may be many difficulties in comprehending reality, but that does not mean that we are without knowledge of it. We are not completely adrift at sea without land in sight; rather, we are anchored securely to a real world that can be understood (in part) by honest

> As we gain greater understanding of the world around us, we should constantly be asking whether our worldview needs adjusting to fit reality.

investigation. That is, reality is not the way we would *like* it to be, or *imagine* it to be, or even the way *we have good reason to think* it is. Instead, reality is the way the world *actually is*. The goal as we go forward, then, is to discover a worldview that is consistent with reality. Taking one step at a time, we will need first to consider the *reality of truth*. If there is no essential truth, then there surely is no correct worldview on which to base our lives. In the next chapter we will look at how a proper understanding of the relationship between truth and reality can lay the groundwork for a sensible worldview. From that point, we will want to know whether there is a "someone" who can reveal to us the fullness of reality.

> **CONSIDER THIS**
> Relying only on our own understanding, we risk replacing the definition of reality with our own incomplete or even invalid worldview, interpreting our observations of the world to correspond to that worldview rather than redefining our worldview according to the way the world *actually* is.

2
The Reality of Truth

"All truths are easy to understand once
they are discovered; the point is to
discover them."
Galileo Galilei

In the previous chapter, we saw evidence that the world is real, that
our understanding of the world is reasonable and consistent with
how we experience it. To say it another way, there is no good reason
to think that the world as we experience it is not real. We also saw
that the whole of reality is much more than what humankind can or
ever will have knowledge of—or be able to comprehend.
Nonetheless, we were able to examine some ideas about reality that
we have some understanding of as if what we were saying was *actually
true*—not true only for me or only for you, but true for all.

But what does it mean for an idea to be true? As we saw earlier,
a statement that is true is "in accord with fact," but what is a fact? It's
an idea about or description of the world that is *consistent with reality as
it actually is*. When people say something is a "fact," they mean that
it's not in dispute; it accords with reality *as it actually is*.

When we thought about reality, we envisioned the whole, an all-
encompassing view of all there is in the world; however, we also
learned that we do not have access to the whole, that we are limited,
living in the reality we are trying to envision. Is truth, then, only a
limited collection of all observations or thoughts about the world that
are true? That seems problematic. Even though *we're* the ones who
ultimately determine which ideas to label as "true" or "fact," with our

limited ability to have an accurate and complete grasp of any aspect of this world, we're certain to get it wrong sometimes. Theories change as experts in various fields gain more knowledge.

Not surprisingly, then, calling something a fact does not make it a fact. There are many beliefs that people sincerely treat as factual that aren't. Fact-checking organizations like Snopes.com exist to identify misstatements, urban legends, and lies, and to confirm the truth. As we learn more, we often find out that what we thought was a fact actually needs some rethinking to bring the idea or statement into line with reality; thus, not all so-called "facts" are true. For example, it used to be a widely held notion that most educated people in the Middle Ages thought the earth was flat.[12] This flat earth myth was popularized in the late 19th century despite it having been well-known and widely accepted that the earth was round since before Eratosthenes, a Greek mathematician, calculated the earth's circumference (with reasonable accuracy) around 240 BC.[13]

On the other hand, we often accept certain ideas to be true (that likely are true), but we have some degree of uncertainty about them. For instance, scientists have good reason to believe that black holes exist even though nobody has ever seen one. Scientists can only observe the *effects* of black holes, so they conclude that they really do exist.

Despite the best efforts of scientists, doctors, mechanics, and the rest of us to establish straightforward factual truth, we live in a world that is not quite so tidy. Most of our understanding falls along a continuum of uncertainty, running from "pure speculation" to "thought to be true" to "pretty sure it's true" to "demonstrated beyond a reasonable doubt" to "fact."

But for some of the beliefs we hold dear, we might not know where they fall on our continuum. There are moral beliefs as well as factual beliefs. Some of them might overlap, but some might not. For example, most people believe it's wrong for someone to not wait their turn in line. But is it *factually true* that it's morally wrong? Is it a moral requirement that people of all cultures at all times should obey? Or are these merely societal mores or personal preferences? What about rape, incest, murder, or other acts of violence? Is there any human activity that's wrong for every person of every culture at all times? What about the Holocaust or other genocidal atrocities? Is it a *factual truth* that they were morally wrong and would always be wrong regardless of the reasons held by those who instigated them or the cultures in which they occurred?

Most of us would agree that there are *some* human actions that are always wrong, even if our reasons for reaching that conclusion might differ. Likewise, there are many gray areas. So how do we determine which (if any) human behaviors are always wrong? The difficulty becomes even greater if we ask whether there are certain behaviors that we *ought always to manifest*, those for which a failure to act would be unacceptable behavior. Would failing to help someone in need of assistance or calling 911 if we witness a serious car crash always be wrong?

The Nature of Truth

In truth, we don't have all the answers we would like to have, and we often don't agree on the correct answers to questions for which we do have answers. Whether we have a firm grasp on truth depends on the degree to which we rightly comprehend reality. If we live as if reality is whatever we want it to be, aren't we doing what children do when they make up fantasy worlds?

We don't need to have perfect knowledge of reality, however, to understand that there are truths that can be known and followed. For instance, if you were to ask me what kind of car I drove, I wouldn't say, "It has a four-cylinder engine, takes unleaded gasoline, and has four small tires and a small trunk." You would know what kinds of cars I did *not* have (those with six- or eight-cylinder engines, for example), but my answer would miss the intent of the original question. A better response would be, "I have a Hyundai." It is the understanding of the "whole" that gives meaning to the "parts." People understand perfectly well what is meant by "car" even if they don't understand all of its mechanisms and the way it works. The same is true for "reality." According to the *Merriam-Webster Dictionary* online, the nature of something is "the inherent character or basic constitution."[14] There is a nature to reality that most of us perceive even if we don't know of the detailed inner workings of the universe; more to the point, *none of us* can claim to have definitive knowledge of more than a small portion of it. Generally speaking, we recognize reality as the "place" in which we live and move, even if we cannot explain how or why we experience it as we do. The same can be said of truth as a right understanding of reality. If we understand the nature of truth—the language by which we describe and understand reality—then we ought to be able to establish some principles that will help us distinguish what is true from the false.

But it's one thing to suggest that the truth can be known; it's quite another to agree on what that truth might be. As we saw in the previous chapter, our personal worldviews can restrict what we will accept as true. For example, there are probably remote places in the world where people have neither seen nor heard of airplanes, so planes do not exist in their worldview. If you traveled to such a place and described to the people how you arrived there, they would have no framework by which to understand and accept your story as truthful. They might not even have a word for "plane." A person's understanding of, and beliefs about, reality (his or her worldview) has serious implications for the range of ideas that he or she will include in a search for truth.

> A person's understanding of, and beliefs about, reality (his or her worldview) has serious implications for the range of ideas that he or she will include in a search for truth.

Every one of us has a worldview: a personal view of reality. Worldviews grow and change over time due to life circumstances, interests, education, abilities, upbringing, culture, religious beliefs, and anything else that might affect our knowledge and understanding. We can easily see that there are as many unique worldviews and as many different *perspectives* on truth as there are people. Perhaps that's why there are many people today who claim that there is no such thing as *absolute* truth; that truth depends on one's personal preference or understanding. If reality can be personal, then truth can also be personal—whatever we want it to be.

But doesn't that say more about us than about the truth?

We come to differing conclusions regarding the truthfulness of a statement or claim because we naturally determine what is true by comparing a truth claim to our personal views of reality. Sometimes we consciously stop to consider what is said, while at other times we come to an immediate conclusion. We call claims that match or correspond to the world as we believe it to be "true" (or "true for us"), and we judge those that fail to do so to be "false" (or "false for us"). But just because we have different worldviews and perceptions, does that mean there are really multiple versions of the truth?

While each of us may have differing understandings or views of reality, *there can only be one reality.* It may be unknown (or unknowable) to us or known only in part, but there isn't a separate reality for every human being. So, when I say that "truth is that which conforms or corresponds to reality," I mean that truth is an accurate description or understanding of the *one and only reality.* If there aren't multiple realities, then there cannot be multiple truths about it, either. Eyewitnesses to a crime sometimes have differing, even conflicting, versions of the events that took place.[15] As a result, investigators must piece together the eyewitness reports with physical evidence to determine what actually occurred—the one consistent explanation of the crime that is true. Consequently, truth—*The Truth*—is not dependent on our perceptions, but, rather, on the way the world *actually is.*

Truth may be understood broadly as that which characterizes reality, an understanding of the whole of reality to the degree we have experienced or have knowledge of it. Our purpose in speaking of truth has been to try to capture certain indispensable, unchangeable ideas or principles that make the world the way it is and help us live within it. In searching for truth, we seek to explain why things are the way they are, venturing beyond questions of fact to questions about existence, such as whether or not things could have been different than they are. Are there other planets that could sustain life or stars like our Sun that could provide the necessary heat and light for life as we know it? Why is there life at all? Thus, we seek truth, not only to know what is (as far as we can tell) but the constraining principles of reality that limit what could be (or could have been).

As we go about seeking truth, we need to understand the pitfalls to human thinking so that we can avoid them when possible and recognize our limitations at all times. To put it more concisely: garbage in, garbage out. After we "inspect the foundation," we will assess whether it is possible to uncover *the truth* solely through the use of human reason. Our challenge is to understand *the way the world actually is* so that we will find *The Truth*—not truth for me or truth for you, but truth for all. For the remainder of this chapter, then, we will consider whether this goal is actually attainable.

A Truth Based on Reason

Human beings have creative intelligence. We are not simply thinking machines, gobbling up data like a computer, processing it according to a certain program, and spitting out answers. We are actually capable of forming thoughts never before considered by ourselves or possibly even by others. It is in our nature to reason like this—to think about, contemplate, and ponder—to grapple with who we are, where we live, and how or why we came to be.

Amazingly, reason allows us to investigate the world, and the world seems to conform with or yield itself to human reason. We find that the world behaves in ways that are consistent with the way we reason, and we reason in ways that are consistent with the way the world works. When we are confronted by some occurrence that seems to defy comprehension, we might be filled with wonder, but we generally hold to the conviction that there must be a reasonable explanation for what we have seen or experienced. Why? In addition to our past experiences and what we have learned, we have what seems to be an inborn awareness that the world in which we live is open to rational examination, appreciation, and understanding, that is, that we can know the world through the use of reason. While we might be baffled by many of the wonders of nature, it is not because they result from irrational or magical processes.[16]

"Rational," however, does not necessarily mean "intuitive." For instance, we know from experience that ice floats in water. We may not think much about that because we are so used to seeing it, but it isn't obvious that ice (a solid) should float. Even so, if we really wanted to find out why, the scientific explanation is readily available.[17] While the way the world works is not always apparent, we hold to the belief that there must be a rational explanation for its structure, mechanisms, and processes. Our experiences in the world can usually be examined and understood in the light of reason.

Clearly, then, there must be a connection between reason and truth; we would not be able to discover what is true apart from reason. Further, reason allows us to connect true ideas to form true principles that can be used to evaluate other claims to truth. On the other hand, it cannot be the case that truth exists solely because we can reason. If that were the case, then truth would be invented whenever we—as individuals or a society—decide that something is true. But we have already established that truth is that which conforms to reality, independent of our ideas about it or the conclusions we reach. And since reality already exists, truth must already exist as well. Thus, reasoning is the human capacity to investigate, discover, and understand the truth in the world—but within the limits of human knowledge and reason.

FOR THE LOVE OF TRUTH

Even scientists do not always reason their way to a correct understanding the first time they encounter a previously unexplained phenomenon. There are many aspects of this world that continue to defy our understanding in every field of study, even after years of investigation. All of us deal with questions of morality and ethics, those standards or guidelines by which we determine whether an action (or inaction) is good or bad, right or wrong. And we all have to navigate through those daily life issues that seem to crop up out of nowhere, often involving relationships, for which the answers are usually not simple. It seems that we have insufficient knowledge and understanding of the world in every aspect of life, from science and technology to the norms of human behavior and relationships, that is, in all facets of reality.

Comprehending the world is like peeling an onion. We deal with one layer of reality at a time, often making several missteps in understanding before arriving at a conclusion. If we're honest with ourselves, *we are constantly changing what we believe to be true* as we realize that previous ideas were incomplete, inaccurate, or wholly wrong.

Truth we can count on may not seem significant if we are talking about theories that have little effect on most of us (like the latest advances in astronomy or physics), but what if you want to know whether a certain medicine will help or harm your children? Parents want to know *the truth* regarding that medicine, not opinions or theories. That is not to discount expert opinion, but no matter how sincere or well-considered, even expert advice can be false in part or in whole.

What if a committee of experts agreed on a particular "truth"? Would that be sufficient to accept an idea as *absolutely true*? No. Multiple specialists do not necessarily make for better results. While they might have a dynamic discussion of ideas until the group reaches some kind of consensus (assuming they reach a consensus), rarely do they arrive at unanimous agreement without someone having to make a concession. Compromise can be useful when choosing among several imperfect alternatives, but it is not what we want if we are serious about finding *the truth*. Again, I am not suggesting we ignore a consensus by experts, but neither should we assume that they are right simply because they are smart, well-educated, or generally agree with one another. Truth goes by a different standard than "the best compromise our brightest minds have to offer."

As thinking beings, it is critical for us that the world functions according to consistent principles. While animals can live in this world quite nicely apart from reason, living by instinct, it is through reason that human beings are able to seek and find truth, however incompletely, and through that truth to navigate the opportunities and challenges in our lives. We cannot think or act apart from accepting or believing that some things about the world—about reality—are true. Otherwise, we would never know what to expect from the world or how to respond to it.

Limitations on Human Reason

We have absorbed many ideas from our experiences and culture without questioning their validity or whether they conform to reality. Just as reality is what it is, so the truth of reality does not change to fit human reason. It's not that truth is unreasonable, but people certainly can be. Sound reasoning yields truthful conclusions only when we start with a solid foundation and then build a structure on that foundation that is also sound.

Truth's Uncertainty Principle

The most apparent obstacle to establishing truth is that we do not always have reliable access to all that we need to know of reality. Our lives are full of ideas or beliefs we take to be true even though we lack sufficient evidence to claim *certain* knowledge, such as some of our beliefs about God. And then there are other ideas and beliefs that we profess to have near-certain knowledge about, but we may be mistaken about them, such as black holes. That is not to say that we are necessarily wrong about these ideas or that we are incapable of knowing anything with certainty, but, rather, that we may be unaware that some of what we think we know and the decisions we make may not be as solidly grounded as we may believe.

Does your spouse go to work every day? Do you have *certain* knowledge of that? In the movie, *True Lies*,[18] Harry Tasker leads a double life as a computer salesman and secret agent, but his wife, Helen, is aware only of his routine, boring sales life. As the movie unfolds and Helen Tasker learns of her husband's real identity, she quips: "When he said, 'I do,' he never said what he did." Obviously, her certainty lacked complete information. Having reasonable certainty is not the same as having perfect knowledge. Despite having a significant amount of evidence, *she did not know with absolute certainty* (as an indisputable fact) what her husband did every day. I'm not suggesting we live in suspicion of our spouses, but the movie exposes the tentative nature of what we call "knowledge." Most of us would say quite confidently that we *"know"* what our spouses do for work. Helen Tasker would have said this as well, but not only did she not know what she didn't know, but what she believed about her husband was actually false.

It's hard to look critically at what we think we know. One of the essential components of knowledge is truth, not what we believe to be true but what is actually true. It may seem obvious that knowledge statements are statements asserting some kind of truth, but we are sometimes unaware that some of what we call "knowledge" is grounded in what we *believe* to be true rather than what we know unquestionably.

Imagine you're watching a movie and early on you suspect someone to be the villain. If, at the end of the movie, that person is indeed revealed to be the villain, what do you typically say? "Ha! I knew it." But do you really mean that you knew for a fact, or do you mean that you had reasons to believe and therefore ventured an educated guess as to the villain's identity? Knowledge is attained in our minds when we have sufficient reasons, or evidence, or justification *to believe* that a certain idea or proposition is true—that our belief conforms to the way the world actually is.

But how are we to decide what is sufficient? In the example above, you believed you had clues enough to give you some measure of confidence, enough to make an educated guess, but why did that belief not amount to knowledge? Because we could easily see and acknowledge that we might be wrong. In the regular concerns of our lives, however, it can be harder to see clearly (and to admit) that we might be wrong. Our beliefs become knowledge for us when we are moved *to act as if what we believe is actually so*, but while you might have guessed correctly who the villain was, you probably wouldn't be willing to bet a lot of money on it (unless you just like to gamble).

What people call "knowledge" is not always undeniably true. We can see this at play in the criminal justice system of the United States. Prosecutors are not required to "prove with absolute certainty" that a defendant committed a crime but, rather, that the defendant's guilt be established "beyond a reasonable doubt," meaning "proof of such a convincing character that you would be willing to rely and act upon it without hesitation in the most important of your own affairs."[19] We don't always get it right (often with tragic consequences), but thankfully, the American judicial system does have means of correcting those injustices.

It can sometimes make us uncomfortable when we realize that what we call "knowledge" is grounded in what we *believe* to be true. Does that not mean that what we think we know is more about our personal or societal beliefs than about reality? Well, yes … and no. If we couldn't trust *anything* we believed to be true about the world, then we'd have a problem. We would have difficulty in life if we refused to accept some notions as factual, or nearly so, and if everything we said to one another had to be prefaced with, "I believe…." But that's not the case. We have direct access to some of the world *as it actually is* and can, therefore, develop reasonable beliefs about reality that we legitimately take to be knowledge.

The trouble is, there's no way to pinpoint when a belief becomes a certainty or even a near-certainty. As a result, there's a sense that anyone can claim at any time to know something "for a fact." Many people accept stated "truth" because of what an "expert" claims for a fact, and often, we believe what we learn from a friend or the internet. I am not discounting the advice or knowledge of experts, friends, or the internet, but experts are not infallible, even in their specific fields of study. *Being an expert is not the same as having perfect knowledge.* If a proposed "fact" cannot be *disproven*, it can become generally accepted as truth, even if there is little evidence or rationale in its support. It can be virtually impossible to prove a negative, that an idea is *not true.* To give a silly example, suppose you told your friends that you turned into a werewolf yesterday (but just for a few minutes). Unless your friends could find eyewitnesses for *every* minute of your past 24 hours, they would find it impossible to prove that your story was false, despite its absurdity. In a similar vein, the Search for Extra-Terrestrial Intelligence (SETI) project continues because those associated with it *believe* that the existence of aliens is likely. Of course, no one can prove otherwise, and there is some evidence of mysterious events on Earth that seem inexplicable on human terms. Thus, the SETI project carries on in the *belief* that it is only a matter of time before we contact extraterrestrial intelligent life. For the SETI folks, it is a near certainty that extraterrestrial intelligent life exists, even though no direct evidence of such life has been found—they would say, "has yet to be found."

On the other hand, we can have thoughts, convictions, or beliefs that are true even if we cannot prove them. Truth exists apart from our knowledge.

None So Blind

What do we do when we find holes or cracks in a foundation? We fill or fix them. Otherwise, we might soon find that water is leaking into our house, a problem that could result in an unsafe structure. The least costly time to fix a crack is when it first appears.

The longer we wait, the worse it can get. Nonetheless, it is not always easy to find the cracks in a foundation, and it may be that we see the effect (water where it shouldn't be) before we realize that a crack exists. The same applies to us. We may not realize that some of the foundational ideas we hold, or principles we live by, are flawed, allowing errant notions to "leak" into our minds, take root, and contaminate the way we think. As the adage goes, "There are none so blind as those that will not see." Consider the following example, which is a true story surrounding one of America's worst spy scandals and the subject of a *60 Minutes* interview.

The Hanssen Espionage Case

The spy was Robert Hanssen, and the man being interviewed was Brian Kelley,[20] the Central Intelligence Agency (CIA) operative who was initially suspected of espionage activities. At the time of the interview, Kelley still worked for the CIA but stated that any hopes of career advancement had been dashed despite having been proven to be innocent. The background information included below is from Wikipedia and the *60 Minutes* special.[21]

Robert Hanssen was an American Federal Bureau of Investigation (FBI) agent who spied for the Soviet Union and Russia against the United States over a 22-year period. Hanssen was arrested on February 18, 2001, charged with selling American secrets to Moscow for more than $1.4 million in cash and diamonds. On July 6, 2001, he pleaded guilty to 15 counts of espionage and was sentenced to life in prison.[22]

The FBI knew that one or more spies were leaking classified intelligence beginning sometime in the late 1980s, but it was not until the late 1990s that agents began to zero in on a suspect, Brian Kelley. The FBI investigators *were certain* that Kelley was their man because there were only a few people who actually had access to the information that had found its way to our adversaries. They didn't even consider the possibility that the spy could be one of their own agents. To test Kelley, they sent a man posing as a foreign operative to tell Kelley that the FBI was onto him, but Kelley did exactly what he was supposed to do, reporting the incident. How did the investigators respond? They told themselves, "This guy's good" (at being a spy, that is). And later, when they interrogated him and his family, he was put through an intensive lie detector test, which he passed with flying colors. How did the investigators react? Again, they told themselves, "This guy's an ice man."[23] The agents were so convinced that they knew the "truth" that Kelley was the spy, they were blinded to the possibility that they could be wrong. As a result, they misinterpreted the evidence that should have led them to question whether they had the right person. Their predetermined assumptions became their reality into which they force-fitted the evidence, rather than following the evidence to the truth.

A bias is a tendency to prefer one idea or choice over or against another, regardless of the available evidence, and it "interferes with the ability to be impartial, unprejudiced, or objective."[24] We all have biases, and it can be hard to identify and see past them; we often fail to realize how or even that they are affecting the way we think. It's not that having a bias will *always* lead to a wrong answer. The FBI in this example *might* have been right, but not because they had properly evaluated the evidence before them. The FBI investigators' refusal to believe that one of their own men might have been a spy caused them to misinterpret or ignore the apparent facts.

We often reveal our personal biases when we express opinions about a matter that are based on the way we believe things are, or the way we would like them to be, *in spite of* available information to the contrary. Bias can blind us to the possibility that we might be wrong. Sometimes, we *intentionally* disregard evidence that contradicts our bias, but many times we are so invested in a particular point of view that our minds are unable to come to terms with ideas that might cause us to reconsider. Consequently, we can fall victim to our personal confirmation bias—only letting in information that supports our existing view. We can read, hear, or even observe with our own eyes, but never *really* see or listen. Our brains register the information or evidence, but we miss or cannot accept its critical application to our beliefs, especially if we have built our lives around those beliefs.

Many of us root for our favorite sports team. But have you ever noticed that the referees or umpires are almost always "wrong" when "our team" is penalized or a play call goes against "us"? Sometimes, we even begin to think of the team as an extension of ourselves, making it all the more difficult to be objective. Unfortunately, the same can be true in more weighty matters. We don't really like it when the results aren't what we expected or hoped for, and we can be tempted to ignore clear evidence or even to "game" the system in a way that influences the result. That's why professionals have codes of conduct and ethics; scientists follow the scientific method; pastors have the Bible; politicians are bound by constitutions; umpires stick to the rulebook; and most of us are beholden to our own code of conduct.

We can also show our bias when we hold onto a personal worldview despite its obvious flaws. While any individual bias can blind us to a particular truth, a worldview colors everything we think, say, and do. As we discussed previously, a worldview is the mind's framework into which we fit those bits of information we take in from the world; it governs how we determine what we believe. A worldview often filters out the notions we simply won't accept as true, short-circuiting the process of investigating whether those ideas might actually conform to reality.

When we're biased toward a particular way of looking at things, we tend to interpret whatever we observe or learn in a manner that confirms our particular viewpoint (as the FBI did in the Hanssen story). So, for example, someone might believe that a moral code is simply something created by, and for the good of, society while another person thinks that there is a fixed morality given from outside of society (e.g., by a moral lawgiver) to which all people and societies are beholden. The former will interpret the fact that a society outlaws the killing of innocent people as an indication that it wants to survive, and such killing would be detrimental to that end. The same person might argue that if morality had been imposed by a moral lawgiver, then all societies would have similar codes of law, but they don't; therefore, morality is not imposed from outside and there is no moral lawgiver. On the other hand, the person who believes that morality is determined outside society will interpret the fact that all societies have some sort of moral code as evidence that we are inherently moral beings obligated to some sort of moral lawgiver. This person will argue that killing innocent people (while "innocent" is defined differently in different cultures) is wrong in virtually all societies because it's *inherently* wrong regardless of whether or not societies pass laws making it illegal.

We can't get away from being biased to some extent. Even if we were robots, we would still be constrained to think according to some predetermined algorithm, which would be programmed by a human with a particular worldview. Over the course of our lives, we develop personal positions and worldviews that we tend to be invested in, and therefore, biased toward. There is, however, a point at which bias becomes unreasonable … and unreasoning. We can even become a little like the monkey who will not let go of some tempting food.[25] As the story goes, in order to catch a monkey, you can put the food in a coconut with a hole just large enough for the monkey's hand. It will grab the food and continue to hang onto it even though it will not be able to pull the hand, together with the food, out through the hole. The monkey will refuse to give up the food even to keep itself from being caught. Indeed, human beings are not all that unlike this monkey when it comes to our biases.

Some of the most sinister threats to the truth are the culturally popular biases that supposedly "everyone knows are true." We don't typically have or take the time to ask whether these beliefs make sense, or perhaps we assume that "everyone" couldn't possibly be wrong. But they can become cultural norms and make their way into our subconscious minds, becoming standards against which future thoughts and actions are measured. We begin to act as if to doubt them would be unthinkable, so much so that it wouldn't be unusual for someone who bucks the trend to be viewed as abnormal or even "evil." "Tolerance" and "political correctness," for example, hold the status of virtues in our society, while people who think otherwise are considered "intolerant" or "bigoted"—ironically, by those who claim to be "tolerant."

As already discussed, the real danger is not so much being biased but in failing to recognize our bias and how it challenges our understanding of reality, leading us toward a worldview that is false. Those of us who have piloted an airplane know that going from Point A to Point B is not as simple as pointing toward Point B and assuming you'll get there. Among other things, the plane will drift off course due to winds that can change its speed and direction. The pilot needs to be constantly vigilant, making appropriate course corrections whenever the inevitable drifting occurs. The same concept applies to the truth. We need to acknowledge the bias that can cause us to drift from the truth and be prepared to correct our views as necessary.

> The real danger is not so much being biased but in failing to recognize our bias and how it challenges our understanding of reality, leading us toward a worldview that is false.

A Guess Is Still a Guess

"Assuming" can get us into trouble as well. Assumptions are often the filler for those parts of reality about which we have limited knowledge. Yet, they play an important role in reason, making it possible for us to make decisions or choices when we lack complete awareness of all the facts. While assumptions can be useful and even necessary, we often fail to realize when we make one, or we miss the implications of having done so.

Assumptions come in different forms. Some assumptions are largely conjectures without much in the way of solid backing; they are often no more than someone's personal opinion, hope, or desire. Other assumptions might be considered "educated guesses," still more guess than certainty, but not without some basis. Take, for example, a situation in which your young daughter comes to you at night because she's heard or seen something outside, and she's frightened. You reassure her, saying something like, "Oh, that was probably just a cat getting into the neighbor's garbage," or "It must've been a tree branch scraping against the house." You make an educated guess knowing that such causes are likely and will help calm your daughter. You could be right, but you can't be *certain*. Educated guesses are often where we begin when trying to solve a problem. So, if your daughter doesn't quite accept your explanation, you could investigate the possible sources of the noise, starting with your guesses, checking out the garbage cans and the tree limbs. Whether your daughter will now return to bed is anybody's guess.

Next is the "reasonable assumption," which is still an assumption but is established on a more solid foundation than the educated guess. Most of us assume that our cars will start when we turn the key. The car wouldn't be of much use if we didn't have reason to make that basic assumption. Can you imagine what it would be like if cars started so randomly that we could never count on them? Before long, we'd switch to a more reliable mode of transportation. But cars aren't like that. The assumption that our new car will start whenever we need it is reasonable. Nevertheless, the mechanical parts eventually wear down, and one day, our not-so-new car may fail to start without warning. Yet, it is both reasonable and useful to assume that it will run for a certain number of years or miles without major problems, which is why cars come with warranties.

By contrast, consider the dot.com craze in the late 1990s. Many people *assumed* that new dot.com internet businesses would flourish, seemingly without limit, and investors made investments resulting in great gains in the stock market.[26] But some investors failed to account for the uncertain timing of the end, but an end that was certain to come. Perhaps they assumed, without thinking much about it, that there was no time limit on the dot.com boon or that they would see the end coming in time to move their money to less risky investments. Unfortunately for them, when the end finally did arrive, it was a crash rather than a slowdown, happening too quickly for speculators to move their investments to more secure stocks. Many people lost all they had gained and perhaps much more. Investors had failed to account for the uncertainty in their investments, the *assumption* that they would have plenty of time to reinvest if necessary.[27]

At its core, an assumption is really just a guess. We may consider an assumption to be "educated" or even "reasonable," but in the final analysis, it is no more than a guess with a greater or lesser degree of confidence. There is no guarantee that the "educated guess" or "reasonable assumption" will lead to the desired outcome. We typically *assume* we are being perfectly reasonable, but every assumption remains little more than speculation. No matter how sensible an idea may seem, good judgment dictates that we be mindful of the possibility that some of our assumptions are wrong.

A Question of Authority

We do not typically come to know the truth we know solely by use of our own reason. Many of the ideas we hold to be true come from what we have read or heard from "experts." Reason may play little or no role in believing them. The fact is, we often accept their statements as true because we recognize their credentials as experts, and we don't generally have the educational background, training, or experience necessary to question (or sometimes even fully understand) what they say. However, as already mentioned, even honorable experts sometimes are in error. In fact, even experts can have limited knowledge within their specific fields of expertise. They may know more about their specialties than we do, but that doesn't mean that their knowledge or understanding of the subject matter is without gaps or errors. The very fact that specialists spend their whole lives researching their chosen subject matters to gain a greater depth of understanding and uncover new truths demonstrates that they lack accurate and complete knowledge even in their fields of study. There would be no reason for them to study or research if they already knew all there was to know about their specialty. Have doctors never changed the guidance they give us regarding what is healthy to eat or drink? Some doctors used to say that smoking was healthy![28] But as they have gained greater insight into the functioning of the human body, they have been able to determine more accurately what constitutes a healthy diet. And that ought to alert us to this reality: No doctor or any other expert has all of the necessary knowledge or understanding to speak with *absolute* authority.

Just as most of us do not have the time, training, or education to verify everything an expert tells us, the same is true for the experts. No one can know everything, and it is especially the case that no one can investigate every idea themselves to arrive at their conclusions. While they may dazzle us with their intellect, even the experts must often rely upon other experts for some (or much) of what they believe to be true. You would not want your eye doctor treating you for cancer, or the podiatrist trying to relieve your toothache.

So where does this leave us? If we cannot unreservedly trust that our experts are right, how are we supposed to establish *the truth*? We are either left to hobble along, crippled by the collective limitations of humanity, or we need to find an authority that can be trusted *absolutely*.

A Time for Truth

What is truth? We established at the beginning of this chapter that truth is a correct description or understanding of reality, but that definition didn't seem very helpful given our inability to fully comprehend reality. Consequently, the same limitations we had in understanding reality applied to those notions we think are true about reality. As a result, we decided to look at the nature of truth as an essential aspect of reality. Distinct from an assembly of facts, perhaps truth could be understood more broadly by capturing principles that could be applied to reality. In this view, our purpose in speaking of truth was to capture certain indispensable, unchangeable ideas or principles that would accurately depict the way the world actually is. In other words, ideas would have a truth nature in themselves, being true or false apart from any human knowledge.

This led us to wonder about the connection between reason and truth. We found that the world certainly seems to be open to our reasoned examination of it, and our reason appears to be compatible with the way the world works. But we also recognized that reason alone does not establish truth. Since reality already exists, the truth about reality must already exist as well. Thus, we determined that reason is the human capacity to investigate, discover, and understand the truth about the world. We also found, however, that while truth may be reasonable, we can't count on human reason to always lead to that truth.

CONSIDER THIS
While truth may be reasonable, we can't count on human reason to always lead to that truth.

We have looked at a number of ways in which our search for truth can be corrupted. Biases, the influence of cultural norms, faulty or unknown assumptions, and over-reliance on experts all hinder us on the way to establishing a firm foundation on which to build a reliable understanding of reality. And then there is the simple uncertainty that results from a flawed or incomplete view or understanding of reality—the way the world actually is. We're not always careful to think deeply about the ideas we hold as true and by which we guide our lives. If much of what we believe to be true is founded on so many uncertainties, how is it we can have any confidence in what we conclude? How is it we can claim to know *the truth* at all?

We know so little about the world in comparison to what there is to know that it's amazing that we're able to come to any certain conclusions about its nature and workings. Either *the truth* is inaccessible to human reason, or there is no ultimate truth. But we have already established that truth is that which conforms to reality and reality exists; therefore, truth must exist. So, where do we go from here? I've suggested a number of times that we cannot fully comprehend reality—and consequently, the fullness of truth—unless "someone" from outside the universe tells us the way the world really is.

Now we have reached the point where we need to ask whether it is conceivable for that "someone" to exist, and if so, whether there is reason to believe that that "someone" has actually communicated the truth to us.

3
The Source of Reality

> "Once you eliminate the impossible,
> whatever remains, no matter how
> improbable, must be the truth."
> Arthur Conan Doyle

Looking for "Someone"

We've touched on this topic a few times, but now it's time to flesh it out. No matter what advancements are made by science or in other fields of study, it's simply a fact that we will never fully understand everything by human reason alone. As someone has asked, "Can a fish know it's wet?" Likewise, we're trapped inside the very world we're trying to explain. But that raises the question of whether or not such a being might exist and, if so, whether that "someone" could tell us anything about this world and ourselves.

Let's begin by asking how the world we live in—the universe—came to be in the first place. Has it always existed, or did it have a beginning? Why begin here? Because if the someone we're looking for had nothing to do with the world's origin, then it seems unlikely that he would be the source of truth we desire.[29] Lesser beings might have some useful knowledge, but only the one who initiated our world would know why he did so and whether we have a purpose in it. But if our world did have a beginning, how can that be explained given our experience that everything that has a beginning has an originating cause? Are we the product of an intelligent mind or the consequence of random natural processes?

> **CONSIDER THIS**
> Unless someone—an intelligent being not bound by our space-time reality—tells us how this world came to be and what our role in it is, we can never be confident that our answers to the important questions of life are anything more than mere speculations.

Unfortunately, since we'll never know all there is to know about this world, we won't be able to definitively answer those questions. We will, however, be able to see that it is *rational* to believe that the universe owes its existence at least in part to an intelligent being of some sort.

Evidence of Intelligence

How did this world come to be? Why does it exist at all? Before we try to answer these questions, let's consider how material objects or life come to be *within* our world. We never experience them coming into existence out of nothing (*ex nihilo*). It might seem that way when, for instance, we have the impression that a flower popped into existence overnight; however, we know that the flower came from a bud that was part of the plant, which came from a seed that came from a plant, and so on. It didn't come from nothing.

We also know a great deal about the way people and animals employ nature's products for protection, food, and shelter. Nature's creatures often re-form or re-purpose the materials available to them, such as when a bird builds a nest or a beaver constructs a dam. The bird and beaver work according to instinct, some internal programming not unlike the programs we use to control computers or robots. The structures of a bird's nest and beaver's dam are complex and exacting, not something that can be mimicked by natural random processes. Only an intelligent being could gather and weave together these homes out of their hundreds or thousands of pieces. If we were walking alongside a river and saw the dam pictured below, would our first thought be that a bunch of driftwood was clogging the river, or would we think that something or someone deliberately put it there for a particular reason?

Figure 1: Random Act of Nature?[30]

Sometimes natural processes leave behind structures that intelligent creatures then utilize for their own purposes, such as naturally formed caves that people or animals discover and use for shelter, but such "creations" are merely accidental. Random natural processes, such as wind or water erosion, earthquakes, and volcanoes, can never intentionally form anything for a specific purpose.

Only intelligent creatures can shape their environment with some goal in mind. And only human beings have the capacity to think rationally (to reason why things are the way they are) and creatively (to envision how things might be different). Our rational capacity and creativity work together to make it possible for us to bring to fruition what we envision. We are not limited by pre-programmed instinctual behaviors. Instead, we can ask and find answers to who, what, when, where, why, and how questions, and we're able to recognize when an answer does not fit the available evidence, or when an answer is unreasonable or illogical.

Our creative nature gives us the capacity to develop new ideas and to mold or craft what we never before imagined, whether in the arts, music, cooking, architecture, technology, or engineering. We even call our products "creations," not because we brought them into existence out of nothing, but because we designed and formed them apart from any blueprint implanted in our brains at birth. We create for a *purpose*, even if only for personal enjoyment or pleasure, designing our creations to fulfill their intended aims. What then of the universe itself? Is it possible that the universe exists of its own necessity—without cause—or could it be the product of a Creative Intelligence with a purpose in mind?

Why There Is Not Nothing

We're born into a world that already exists, so it rarely occurs to most people that it could be otherwise—that there could have been nothing instead of something. Of course, there wouldn't be anyone to ask why there is not nothing if there really was nothing, and most of us first learn from our parents whatever they believe to be true, that "God created the world," or "The world has always been here." But maybe we wonder if there's a more certain answer.

No matter how much we are able to discover or theorize about our past, we will never know with absolute certainty how the universe came to be—*because we weren't there*. And that means that whatever explanation we accept as true, we cannot eliminate faith as an element in our determination. In fact, as we've already suggested, there are few ideas that we commonly take to be true for which we have absolute certainty; belief is an unavoidable aspect of knowledge that we seldom consider. Regardless of the explanation we accept for the existence of the world, our understanding is necessarily grounded in an unprovable assertion about its origin, a claim that is little more than formalized belief. Nonetheless, we can still ask whether there is a "best" explanation, one that is more plausible than any other.

But where should we start? Dr. William Lane Craig modernizes an argument first put forth by Dr. Gottfried Wilhelm Leibniz (1646-1716)[31] that one way to begin is by asking why there is "something rather than nothing."[32] Surely, it is possible that the universe might not ever have existed, but what could explain the fact that it *does* exist?

According to Leibniz, the explanation of something's existence "may be found *either* in the necessity of a thing's nature or else in some external cause."[33] So, one approach is to say that the universe exists because it had to—there is only one form that the components of the universe could have taken, and that's the configuration of our current universe. The pieces of the universe *necessarily* exist in this arrangement because they couldn't exist any other way. On this view, then, no explanation is required—there's no "before the universe existed." It simply "is." There's no need to imply that a creator made the universe. To say it another way, if the universe exists inexplicably, then there's no need for a god.

But even atheists acknowledge the problem of suggesting that the universe could not have been any way other than it is—that its elementary particles *had to* come together in the exact structure and with the properties we now know through discovery and investigation.[34] To our knowledge, there is no power or law in the physical world that could have compelled the elements of the universe to cohere in exactly the configuration that now exists. So, if the universe cannot be said to exist inexplicably, what could be the explanation for its existence? With the failure of the argument that it arose from necessity, we're left with no plausible physical—that is, material—explanation.[35]

So, not having any means of explaining the existence of the universe as a necessary product of our *material* world, the only alternative is to consider the possibility that the universe was brought into existence as an intentional act, by an intelligent *immaterial* being having sufficient power and wisdom to cause the world to exist. But what kind of entity would fit this description? It can't be a *creature*, meaning "a created *material* being," because that would require a greater uncreated being to bring the created being into existence. Consequently, the being we're looking for would be the *greatest* uncreated being—an immaterial being whom we may call "God." Thus, if there is an explanation for the existence of the universe, then theism is likely true.

But then, what caused God to exist? Leibniz argues that God exists necessarily, that is, the nature of God is such that it would be impossible for him not to exist.[36] While this statement may sound presumptuous, "even the atheist recognizes [that] it is impossible for God to have a cause."[37] Therefore, *if God exists*, he must exist *necessarily*. The only explanation for God's existence would be the impossibility of some other being greater than God.[38] Since the atheist is unable to provide a plausible explanation for the universe apart from God, that suggests that it is more plausible than not that the explanation of the universe is God.[39]

But who is this creator? Per Craig, "[Leibniz's] argument implies that 'God' is an uncaused, unembodied Mind who transcends the physical universe and even space and time themselves and who exists necessarily,"[40] and who has the capacity to bring the universe into being. This God would have the knowledge to be the "someone" we have been looking for who might be able to tell us what we need to know about the world. Still, we have additional investigating to do, to ensure we are on the right track and, if so, to find out whether this God has in any way made himself known to us. We will look at that in Chapter 5, but before we go there, let's finish our discussion about this world, how it—and the life it supports—came to be.

The First Cause

Throughout history, people have commonly attributed the cause of many natural events to one or many gods. However, we now know that most of the events we observe or experience can be explained as the products of naturally occurring actions.

To be fair, it was not completely without warrant for people living prior to the advent of modern science to speculate that the gods or God might have had *something* to do with all that occurs in our world, including its very existence.[41] Aren't we all awed by the night sky when no city lights dull its incredible vastness and beauty, or by earthquakes, volcanoes, or violent storms? Is it so surprising that people might wonder whether there is a "someone" behind the curtain, pulling the strings, and who that someone might be?

But if Craig and Leibniz are correct, what does it mean for God to be the explanation for the universe's existence? Is his role active or passive? Is God unaware of, and unconcerned with, the universe and us? If philosophical arguments were all we had to go on to answer this question, then the atheist might have justification for ignoring God altogether. In fact, scientists have been so successful at unraveling the complexities of nature over the past several centuries that many of them believe that *everything* we experience or observe will eventually be explained apart from any evidence of God's active participation. On the other hand, we have discovered something special about this world: that the universe had a beginning, *that it began to exist.* In the first quarter of the 20th century, scientists were confronted with this possibility through a prediction of Einstein's General Theory of Relativity, that the universe may not be in a static (unchanging) state as scientists thought, but that it should be expanding.[42] But an expanding universe is one that cannot be eternal. Expansion has to occur from something originally smaller (like when we blow up a balloon), and that means that the universe had a starting point—a beginning—from which it expanded to its present size.[43]

Even kids know from experience that everything that happens has a cause (even if they don't know what it is or don't want to confess that they were the cause!). What about something that begins to exist, that was not in existence at one moment and then suddenly was? Craig uses the prediction of General Relativity—that the universe had a beginning—as support for his Kalam Cosmological Argument (KCA), summarized here:[44]

- *Premise 1: Whatever begins to exist has a cause.*
- *Premise 2: The universe began to exist.*
- *Conclusion: The universe has a cause.*

As Craig states, Premise 1 is hard to argue with since the alternative is the impossibility of something coming into being out of nothing and having no causal agent.[45] As was previously discussed, God did not begin to exist but is eternal, existing necessarily. Justification for Premise 2 comes from both scientific evidence (such as, the expanding universe) and philosophical arguments.[46] Given the truth of the two premises, the conclusion is unavoidable. But it leads us to ask what the cause of the universe could possibly be.

Craig concludes that the cause of the universe must be uncaused. Furthermore,

> ...there are only two sorts of things that could fit that description: either an abstract object like a number or else an unembodied mind. But abstract objects cannot cause anything....So, the cause of the existence of the universe must be a transcendent Mind, which is what [many] understand God to be.[47]

Other theories have been proposed in an attempt to circumvent the implications of a universe that began to exist (that is, one that would require a creator),[48] but they all have at least one fundamental flaw, whatever their scientific merit: They still require the eternal presence of some *thing*, that is, they are all variations on the theme of an eternal, self-existing universe.[49] Even though it cannot be scientifically proven that the universe had a beginning, the best explanation from the available evidence—evidence that continues to mount—favors a universe that was brought into being.

The answer may not be the one we want, but there is a difference between honest skepticism and rigidly refusing to accept plausible results solely because the implications don't confirm our existing beliefs. Truth does not change to fit our desires. Science largely points to a universe that suddenly came into being sometime in the past, and reason leads us to conclude that it must be the work of some preexisting, incredibly powerful being.[50]

CONSIDER THIS

There is a difference between honest skepticism and rigidly refusing to accept plausible results solely because the implications don't confirm our existing beliefs.
Truth does not change to fit our desires.

But isn't it just as hard to comprehend a self-existing eternal God as it is to believe in a self-existing eternal material universe? Both are incomprehensible to our finite human minds. Yet, a self-existing eternal universe is not consistent with science or reason, whereas a self-existing eternal God violates neither. And God has an advantage: A material world cannot purposefully initiate any action, but that's not a problem for an intelligent being. An intelligent God could choose to act (or not act), to envision a design, and then to execute a plan. Thus, even if we cannot fully grasp the notion of a self-existing eternal God, the possibility of an intelligent being intentionally creating our world does indeed conform to human reason and experience. There is nothing we know from either philosophy or science that inherently contradicts the possibility of God as Creator.

Made for Us

Is there a relationship between God and the world he caused to exist? We've already established that the eternal, self-existing Creator is not dependent on the material world for his existence. Therefore, while God exists necessarily, the world exists at God's pleasure— only so long as he chooses to keep it in existence. Consequently, it seems reasonable that there would be a connection of some sort between God and the universe he created. Just as with our own creations, we would expect the universe to reflect the character and purposes of God as well as any effects of his intervention in the world. But do we find evidence *in* this world pointing to its Creator?

Do we have reason to think there is a plan for the universe? That what might appear random might actually be a well-thought-out design? Scientists have begun to see in the very structure of the universe indications that it was created explicitly for human habitation.[51] Known as the Anthropic Principle, scientists have discovered more than 800 fundamental properties of the universe that were so finely tuned when the universe began that even a minor change to just one of those properties would have made this planet unfit for human habitation.[52] In fact, the likelihood of a planet like Earth coming into existence strictly by chance (that is, apart from intelligent intentionality) is less than one in ten to the one-thousandth power (that is, a one followed by 1,000 zeroes!),[53] a probability so small that it is more likely for someone to win the Mega Millions Powerball Lottery approximately 120 times in a row![54] And yet, not only is Earth perfectly suited for human survival, it also happens to be situated in a near-perfect location in the solar system to permit scientific study of the universe.[55] The Anthropic Principle is not only further scientific evidence in support of a creator God, but it is just the type of circumstantial evidence we would expect to find if God purposely created the universe with humans (and animals and vegetation) in mind.

The Life-Giver

In a sense, the universe is only the stage on which a greater mystery is unfolding: the existence and diversity of all life, especially that of humankind. While science and philosophy point to an intelligent, supernatural being who apparently brought the universe into existence and has sustained it, some scientists believe that the evidence points to the life that inhabits Earth coming into being by virtue of strictly natural processes—random changes in organisms accumulating to form every kind of life that has ever existed, including the first. Commonly referred to as "evolution," we now need to look closely at this theory, to see whether the evidence is sufficient to conclude that however we got here, God "sat on the sidelines" during life's development.

4
Evolutionary Dissent

> "Words differently arranged
> have a different meaning,
> and meanings differently arranged
> have different effects."
> Blaise Pascal

Evolution Defined

One of the difficulties surrounding the discussion of evolution is that the term has several different meanings, all of which have been used at one time or another (see Appendix A: The Evolution of Darwinism for an explanation of the origins of evolutionary theory). In its plainest form, "evolution" is just another word for "change," especially of living things. People and animals are born, mature and reproduce according to their natures, and eventually die; so also do plants and trees develop and reproduce according to their natures. All living things evolve in one way or another.

Adaptation (Microevolution)

"Adaptation" is another form of evolution, where certain functional or structural changes occur that are adjustments (adaptations) to a creature's surroundings. Some adaptations are inherent in the nature of the creature, such as the way chameleons can change color to disguise themselves; some are the result of selective breeding by humans or environmental constraints; and some adaptations are the result of **mutations**[56] to a creature's genetic code that are inherited by subsequent generations.[57]

> **MUTATION**
>
> A change to an organism's genetic code, most often due to a replication error occurring during cell division

Professional breeders artificially restrict the populations of animals or plants to those with preferred genetic traits to produce (breed) the variations that meet their needs. For example, show dogs and racehorses are bred for the particular characteristics that will make them winners. Similarly, people who enjoy growing flowers might breed prize roses. And, of course, nature can and does breed varieties on its own without the intervention of humans; **natural selection** favors the propagation of creatures with characteristics that are most suited to survival in their immediate environment.[58] Consequently, this natural process is also referred to as "survival of the fittest."[59]

> **NATURAL SELECTION**
>
> Also known as "survival of the fittest," the observation that the living things most adapted to their environmental conditions tend to survive and reproduce best

Adaptations or variations are also caused by mutations, such as those we observe in "human hair color, skin color, height, shape, behavior, and susceptibility to disease."[60] Since adaptation is responsible only for the variations that we observe among the same *kinds* or *families* of living things,[61] it's also referred to as "*micro*evolution." Even if adaptation produces some fascinating varieties, it does not change the *essential* characteristics that distinguish one family of living things from another. As a result, the changes are considered minor (or micro), not in the sense of being insignificant, but in comparison to the changes anticipated by the third sense of evolution, Darwinism[62] or *macro*evolution.

Darwinism (Macroevolution)

"Darwinism" or "macroevolution" is the most controversial sense of evolution. As the term suggests, *macro*evolution is change on a grand scale, the development and transformation of the first organism[63] into *every* other family of living thing that has ever existed *solely* by natural

INTELLIGENT AGENT

An agent (animal, person, or other being) with the intelligence to envision a desired outcome and cause it to be realized

means (apart from any intervention or influence by an **intelligent agent**[64]). Macroevolution predicts that all living things arose during what is thought to be the 4.54 billion years of Earth's history[65] through the accumulation of millions upon millions of small, adaptive (microevolutionary) changes. For example, according to macroevolutionary theory, the earliest single-celled organisms eventually evolved into dinosaurs through a multitude of intermediate families of living things—and ultimately (for one branch of the evolutionary tree) from dinosaurs through other intermediate forms into today's birds.[66]

Table 1 offers a summary of the concepts.

Term	Also Known As	Cause	Result
Evolution	Change	Aging, wear	Change over time
Adaptation	Microevolution	Breeding, mutations	Variations of characteristics within the same families
Darwinism	Macroevolution	Mutations	New kinds or families of creatures

Table 1: Evolutionary Terms

Common Descent

A logical inference of macroevolution, referred to as **common descent**, is the theory that *all* life forms descended from the first single-celled organism.[67] The theory addresses both the *method* of biological change and the *magnitude* or *extent* of change.

COMMON DESCENT

The common ancestor of *all* life forms is the first single-celled organism

Regarding the method, common descent is grounded in the belief that *natural* or *undirected*[68] biological processes alone are sufficient to explain the development of life; there is no break in the lineage from the first life form to all others that have ever existed—the magnitude —because every new life form is a biological descendant of earlier ones.

UNDIRECTED
Not guided by an intelligent agent; having no purposed goal

Common descent presupposes that there is no biological process that might restrict the cumulative effect of *random*[69] changes due to inherited genetic mutations (microevolution), thus limiting the extent of possible change. Putting these two elements together, we can restate common descent (*macro*evolution) as the theory that *undirected* biological processes acting on *random* genetic changes are sufficient to

RANDOM
Lacking a definite plan, purpose, or pattern

bring about the development and divergence of *all* life forms from the first single-celled organism. But what do we find? Is common descent an adequate scientific explanation for life on planet Earth?

Evolution as the Only Acceptable Scientific Explanation?

Evolutionists tend to generate confusion when speaking in defense of evolution without distinguishing what is known for certain (or nearly so) from what is believed to be so. In my experience, it is not uncommon to read something by an evolutionist stating outright that evolution *must* be true, or is a *fact*, when the evidence presented supports mere adaptation, not transformation from one family into another family.[70] For instance, while we have a great deal of experience with viruses mutating into different forms of the same virus (remember the numerous variations of COVID-19?), to our knowledge, no virus has ever become a different kind of organism altogether. In fact, no one has ever actually witnessed one kind of creature becoming an entirely different kind of creature. A *core assumption* of Darwinism, however, is that every life form *must have* arisen solely by virtue of natural biological processes, but natural selection acting on adaptive variations is the only natural process known to preserve change in biological organisms. Therefore, Darwinian evolutionists have no choice but to assert that adaptation (microevolution) is sufficient to accomplish all necessary modifications (macroevolution) to "create" new families of creatures—all that is needed is a significant amount of time.

Virtually all scientists agree that there is no reason to invoke any type of supernatural intervention (such as a Creator) where natural processes can satisfactorily explain what is observed in nature. And most of us would agree that scientists shouldn't fabricate knowledge as a placeholder for what they don't yet understand. We often think along similar lines. For example, when you hear a crash in the living room and your children say, "That was nothing!" do you think, "I wonder if it was a ghost"? No, you *know* your children (or cat) did something to cause the crash; it wouldn't even occur to you that there might have been Divine intervention. We automatically seek natural explanations for life's experiences; similarly, good science avoids jumping to a "God-of-the-Gaps" solution to explain what we don't know.[71]

Just as scientists need to avoid deferring to the God-of-the-Gaps to explain mysteries, we need to be equally cautious of *refusing* to even consider the possibility that God might have had something to do with the creation and development of life. Even though we seek natural explanations, we also (as intelligent beings) detect the actions of other intelligent beings, just as Mom, in our example, somehow knows that items in the living room do not typically fall over without a little help. It's important to see where the evidence leads before eliminating (or assuming) God as a possible cause of life.

Evolution as an Explanation of the Fossil Record?

Darwin's understanding of breeding techniques and their results, along with his study of the innumerable varieties of living things, ultimately led him to envision natural selection as the controlling mechanism of biological variation. It was the fossil record, however, that caused him to speculate that there was no limit to the amount of change that could take place. It was not an unreasonable hypothesis, especially for his time. A cursory examination of the fossil record can leave the impression that organisms generally progressed over time from simpler to more complex, and from one kind to another. But how convincing is the evidence?

Missing Links

If life were to evolve randomly, having no particular need to change at all, let alone to change in any particular direction, then we would expect evolution to have occurred painstakingly slowly from a single-celled organism (like an amoeba) to a human being. And that expectation leads to another: If an organism really does undergo transformation over millions of years from one family of life form into an entirely different family, we should expect to find a nearly uninterrupted sequence of fossil remains in which every significant structural change required for the transformation is clearly visible in the fossil record.

> **CONSIDER THIS**
> If an organism really does undergo transformation over millions of years from one family of life form into an entirely different family, we should expect to find a nearly uninterrupted sequence of fossil remains in which every significant structural change required for the transformation is clearly visible in the fossil record.

With the exception of fossils not yet discovered, we should have in the fossil record an unbroken chain of so-called **transitional forms**, connecting every life form that exists today (or is now extinct) with its ancestors, all the way back to the organism(s) that were first able to become fossilized.[72] We sometimes

TRANSITIONAL FORMS

Fossils in the chain of development from some extinct creature to its modern form hear that scientists have discovered "*The* Missing Link," but Darwinian evolutionists are not in need of one or even several missing links; *if macroevolution is true, then there needs to be thousands upon thousands, perhaps millions upon millions, of missing fossil links in the chain of change!*

Darwin knew that would have to be the case; he assumed that the fossil record was there but merely incomplete and would be filled in as more fossils were discovered.[73] Some might call that Darwin's "Evolution-of-the-Gaps." His optimism, however, was unwarranted. Now, more than one hundred and fifty years later, the fossil record *is* far more extensive than in Darwin's day, but Darwin's problem has only become worse.[74] While fossils generally increase in size and complexity throughout the historical record (the so-called "geologic column"), we find them in clumps, grouped around major families.[75] The transitional forms between families are still missing.

In fact, attempts by scientists to postulate sequences of transformative fossils have not been convincing. To begin with, the suggested missing links are *always* the fossils of once fully functioning life forms; that is, they are not "part this and part that" but wholly integrated creatures whose body structures and organs were dedicated to and under the control of the creatures' intelligence.[76] Even today's creatures that are capable of surviving in two different environments, such as amphibians, have body structures and organs that are fully compatible with their multi-environment lifestyles.

By contrast, the evolutionist will argue that natural selection only promotes changes that are *improvements* to a creature's ability to survive, that it is to be expected that the surviving creatures are the ones making full use of their changing body structures, and that only the surviving creatures are around long enough to be represented in the fossil record. But that response overlooks an important aspect of macroevolution: Change occurs slowly, in imperceptible steps. No sea-dweller or land-dweller can give birth to an amphibian. It's hard to imagine *any* evolutionary scenario in which the transforming creature would not have to endure a great many generations of partially formed body structures and partially capable organs, an ongoing state of affairs that would almost certainly *not* be advantageous to the creature's survival.[77] Changes that could *eventually* improve individual body structures and organs are not likely to be beneficial to the organism until many other compatible changes are made to compensate for the initial modifications to the body plan. It is difficult to envision even one of the scenarios proposed by Darwinists: how dinosaurs could have evolved into birds through millions of microevolutionary changes.[78] Each change would have to have been beneficial to the survival of the creature such that the change would persist in its offspring *while* the transitioning dinosaur-becoming-bird is not eaten by the non-transitioning dinosaurs before it's able to fly to safety. The evolutionist needs to demonstrate (not merely claim or imagine) that one creature can be transformed into an entirely new creature *without* going through periods when the creature's survival is at risk. There is no known biological process that would ensure otherwise, that the developing creature would be safe from predators during its most vulnerable periods of growth into a new organism. And since we do not find fossils in partially evolved states, we have to wonder whether the fossil evidence actually supports the evolutionary view of life's development at all.

Despite these issues, we still need to consider the evidence presented by evolutionists *for* transitional forms. The University of California Museum of Paleontology in Berkeley hosts a website dedicated to teaching evolution, and it provides two examples of transitional forms:[79]

1. Pakicetus-to-Gray Whale

Beginning with the Pakicetus, a "tiny ... four-footed"[80] land animal that lived some 50 million years ago (mya), we are told that an extinct whale called an "Aetiocetus" (25 mya) is a transitional form between the Pakicetus and our modern gray whale.[81] The evidence provided is that a nostril hole (found in the fossil skulls of the ancient creatures) has migrated from a position near the front of the skull in the Pakicetus, to mid-skull in the Aetiocetus, and finally to the top of the skull (near the eyes) in the modern gray whale.[82] Moreover, we are told that the Pakicetus is "closely related to whales and dolphins" because they share certain unique ear characteristics.[83]

Now, let's perform a lay evaluation of this evidence, beginning with what we ought to affirm. It *is* a curiosity that the skull structures of the Pakicetus, Aetiocetus, and gray whale have similar shapes, and that they all have nostril holes in three different, possibly progressive, positions. Inquisitive people—and scientists generally fit into that category—would typically ask why there are similarities and whether the creatures have some biological connection to one another. And the same can be said of the unusual ear structure shared by the Pakicetus, whales, and dolphins. Scientists ought to investigate why such likenesses exist.

It is not with the questions that we ought to take issue, rather, but with the conclusions, especially when the conclusions are set forth as fact rather than hypothesis. Does the evidence presented validate the claim that macroevolution has occurred in this case? No. Notice that there are no new structures formed in the proposed evolutionary chain. The structures either remain the same or are only slightly modified. Not only that, but there are 25 million years separating each major organism in this chain, and the vast anatomical changes needed to transform a Pakicetus into a whale—which were not discussed on the website—cannot be justified by simply pointing to the alleged migration of a nostril. Nor is there any justification provided (apart from appearance) for claiming that the uniquely similar ears of the Pakicetus and whale could only have resulted from this (or any other) evolutionary chain. Why couldn't they simply be three different creatures that came into existence independently of each other? It is only because the truth of macroevolution is *assumed* that the similar nostril and ear configurations of these creatures is used to "prove" common ancestry.

But let's consider what we would expect to find if macroevolution were true: Conservatively estimating that it would take some 10,000 years on average for gradually developing significant structural changes to become observable in fossil remains, we would expect to see new transitional-form body structures for every 10,000 years of the fossil record during the 50 million years required for the complete transition from Pakicetus to gray whale. Consequently, we should be able to find at least 5,000 conspicuous Pakicetus-to-gray whale transitional forms (50 million divided by 10,000)—2,500 transitional forms for the 25-million-year transition of Pakicetus to Aetiocetus, and the same for the transition to the modern whale. There are thousands of missing links that have yet to be found and verified before it can reasonably be argued that the nostril migration and ear structure correspondence occurred *as part of the transformation of the Pakicetus into a whale.* The evidence we actually have is barely sufficient to provide the basis for a preliminary hypothesis proposing the possibility of evolution, much less validating such an assertion. The potential relationship of the Pakicetus to the gray whale is not nearly as "close" as is being suggested. Perhaps Example #2 will be a more certain example of evolution.

2. Eohippus-to-Equus

This second example documents the macroevolution of the horse's hoof. According to the Museum's website, the four-toed Eohippus evolved over the course of some 50 million years into the single-toed Equus.[84] Even if we accept as a plausible hypothesis that horse toes evolved from Eohippus (originating 55 mya) to Equus (living 4 mya) through various intermediate horse-like creatures, we have to ask what sort of evolution that would represent. The first thing to notice is that the process began with a *four*-toed creature and ended with a *single*-toed creature. There was not any development of a new, previously nonexistent, structure. More to the point, there was a *loss* of three toes. The evolution presented in this case is of the type that can easily be explained by adaptation, as adapting creatures no longer needed all four toes, losing one at a time or all three at once. Since capability was lost, not gained, this example is the opposite of what would be required as an initial step in a macroevolutionary transformation.

Macroevolution or Creation?

Interestingly, neither example validates Darwinian evolution. In fact, it's a good example of how some scientists seem to use micro- and macroevolution interchangeably. These examples were chosen by museum staff out of the "many examples of transitional features"[85] in the fossil record, presumably as two of the most clear-cut instances! Doubling down on that claim, they say that the transitional forms "[provide] an abundance of evidence for evolutionary change over time."[86] The problem is, no one denies that all living things change over time, but significant and species-changing evidence is required. Transformational change from one family of organisms into an entirely new family is what the Darwinian evolutionist needs to demonstrate, and the given examples fail completely on that count.

But suppose the Pakicetus (in the first example) was an entirely separate creation from the Aetiocetus or the gray whale. What then would we make of the evidence? That is, would the evidence fit a creation model? Consider the external similarities. The fact that the general skull structure of the Pakicetus is similar to the Aetiocetus and to the gray whale makes perfect sense on a creation model. We would expect to see a good design reused in a variety of ways by an intelligent creator, in the same way that engineers reuse good designs. More than that, just as engineers tweak those designs for new purposes, we would expect a creator to incorporate modifications in the designs to accommodate similar but slightly different applications. After all, "There's no need to reinvent the wheel." A creator's reuse of a sound design could easily explain the variety of nostril placements on the skulls of the Pakicetus, Aetiocetus, and modern gray whale.

Purpose becomes critically important with this view—the possibility that each and every feature of a creature exists for a specific reason. It would not be surprising to find the same specialized ears on the Pakicetus and the gray whale if they have the same or a similar purpose. While I am not suggesting that the failure of evolution to adequately explain the fossil record proves that life was created or that this evidence is unquestionably in support of creation, the truth is that Darwin's missing links are still missing, and a creator doesn't need them.

The Cambrian Explosion

Even more of a problem for evolution is the "Cambrian Explosion," which is an event in Earth's history dating to approximately 550 mya. At that time, most (over 95%) of the major distinct body structures or **phyla**[87] of the earth came into being "suddenly" during the same short span of time—short, that is, from a geologic and evolutionary standpoint (5 million to 10 million years)—in contradiction to the gradual development required by macroevolution (tens-to-hundreds of millions of years).[88] In addition, no evidence has yet been found in the fossil record of *any* transitional forms that would link the development of the distinct body plans or morphological features to one another.[89]

> ### PHYLUM
> The assemblage of biological species on the basis of general body plan

> ### MORPHOLOGY
> The study of the shapes and arrangement of parts of organisms, in order to determine their function and development

This supports the conclusion that the major phyla developed separately at the same time rather than sequentially, in contradiction of common descent but consistent with what would be expected if the body plans were created.[90]

Punctuated Equilibrium

The Cambrian Explosion presents a real problem for macroevolution. Darwin knew it could disprove his theory if the transitional forms could not be found, but he anticipated their discovery as the fossil record became more complete.[91] As was previously discussed, however, the transitional forms still have not been found. Aware of this problem, Niles Eldredge and Stephen J. Gould developed a new theory in 1972 to explain and mitigate the concerns raised by the Cambrian Explosion, called "Punctuated Equilibrium."[92] They theorized that evolution might not be a process of steady, gradual change (at least not always), but rather one of long periods of little or no change (stasis or *equilibrium*) interrupted (*punctuated*) by geologically short periods of rapid change, during which conditions were especially favorable to the types of mutations that would transform organisms from one body structure into another.[93] If they were right, then it would not be surprising for intermediate fossil forms to be absent from the fossil record, or for the fossil record to give the *impression* that the major body plans developed side by side rather than from a common ancestor. The transitional forms would have been living for a much shorter duration of time than either the initial or final forms, thus vastly reducing the likelihood of being fossilized.[94] It would be like looking for a needle (a comparatively few existing transitional forms) in a haystack (a mother lode of major distinct life forms deposited over hundreds of millions of years).

The concept of Punctuated Equilibrium protects macroevolution from just about every assault that might be mounted against it when dealing with the evidence from the fossil record. But does it actually explain anything, or does it, instead, knit together a camouflage of unfounded and unprovable assertions? What evidence do biologists have that there are *any* conditions that favor the production of benign transformational mutations of life forms?

Mutations can affect an organism in different ways; they can be harmful, have little or no effect (benign), or they can improve the organism in some small way. Benign transformational mutations are the unharmful mutations that would be needed in abundance to transform an organism from one kind of creature into an entirely different family of living being. But most mutations are harmful, and those that are beneficial are generally lost before any significant transformation can occur.[95] The fact is, scientists know of no environment—not even an artificially created one—that can cause an organism to generate benign mutations, much less an environment that *accelerates* the production of beneficial mutations and subsequent transformation of one organism into an entirely different family of life form.[96]

As we have discussed, since there is nothing directing macroevolution toward a particular end, to suggest that certain creatures remained largely unchanged for millions of years and then suddenly began to accumulate random mutations in such a way as to build completely new and more complex creatures "overnight" is simply wishful thinking. Instead, such a transformation suggests intelligent intent, not random, undirected natural processes. Consequently, Punctuated Equilibrium can hardly be considered an adequate explanation for the Cambrian Explosion. The only thing we learn from this hypothesis is what we already know: Evolution might occur quickly, slowly, or not at all!

No doubt, some now well-established theories began with a wild guess by a creative scientist, but those conjectures could not be accepted as valid theories until they were verified by tests, further observations, and/or additional data that support the theories' hypotheses. While Punctuated Equilibrium may be an imaginative *hypothesis*, it cannot be viewed as a satisfactory explanation for the Cambrian Explosion because it succeeds only in changing the nature of the problem:

from the failure of the fossil record to support the standard evolutionary paradigm of continuous, gradual change,

to the inadequacy of any known environmental or biological conditions that could contribute to hundreds of millions of years of minimal change followed by a sudden tendency for the next several (or more) million years to *actively promote* major transformational changes.

On the other hand, the Cambrian Explosion makes perfect sense if a creator intervened at one or more stages in the development of life, causing new life forms to suddenly emerge, even in the blink of an eye.

Macroevolution as the Creator of New Biological Systems?

Darwin knew that animals could be bred, and he correctly theorized that the same mechanism at work in breeding was at work in nature to bring about minor variations or adaptations in living things.[97] He had studied finches in the Galápagos Islands and concluded that the variations they exhibited were the result of adaptation,[98] but his only evidence for large-scale change was the fossil record—which we have seen is unconvincing. Darwin himself registered concern over it: "The several difficulties here discussed [regarding the lack of transitional forms in the fossil record], are all undoubtedly of the gravest nature."[99] It was not until scientists began to understand genetics, and especially when deoxyribonucleic acid (DNA) was discovered,[100] that biologists believed that they finally had the key to explaining macroevolution despite the absence of transitional fossils.[101] Like a modern computer program unique in every living thing, DNA determines how an organism will grow and function. In theory, if random mutations were to "tweak" DNA instructions a little bit at a time over thousands of generations, then entirely new families of organisms might eventually be formed.

The problem is that DNA is not just a random collection of code pieces (DNA base pairs); it is a complex system, similar in construction to a modern computer program but "far, far more advanced than any software we have ever created," according to Bill Gates (founder of Microsoft, writing about human DNA).[102] Consequently, it is not at all clear how the accumulation of minor random improvements (adaptations) could accomplish the wholesale transformation of the DNA instruction sets required to yield whole new body plans. To say it another way, organisms are made up of integrated (connected or networked) cells, structures, and organs, all operating as a system in highly refined coordination.[103] Transforming one organism into another one having entirely different organs and structures, while ensuring that the ever-new organism continues to function as an integrated whole at every step—even having ever-improving survivability—is a task that stretches the limits of believability (and of biology).

The following example provides some indication of the magnitude of the challenge for macroevolution. The DNA of a symbiotic bacterium, *Carsonella ruddii*, contains some 160,000 base pairs,[104] whereas the DNA of humans is approximately 6.4 billion base pairs long.[105] If macroevolution is true, then humans *must* have evolved from that bacterium or something even smaller in size by the accumulation of beneficial, transformational random mutations.[106] Why? In an evolutionary scenario for the development of life, every living thing is linked to the earliest living thing by an unbroken chain of mutations passed from parents to offspring for many generations (common descent). There might be many types of life sprouting from the earliest forms and producing many different families of creatures along the way, but a chain of changes all the way back to the root organisms must connect them all. Therefore, this bacterium or an organism of similar size must have been an early predecessor of human beings. Consequently, the bacterium-sized DNA would need to have *beneficially* mutated *billions* of times, *adding* new DNA base pairs in exactly the right sequence and positions to achieve the requisite 6.4 billion base pairs necessary to be correctly coded for humans. And that does not account for the need to reorder or modify existing base pairs (that is, to adjust the programming or coding) as the organism's structures and functions change[107]—as it becomes one family of living things and then another, slowly progressing through what would have to be millions upon millions of intermediate forms. But where would the transforming mutations gain the "massive amounts of new functional information" needed to produce evermore complex organisms?[108] The Second Law of Thermodynamics is usually applied to physical processes but applies equally to living organisms. It suggests that biological systems should naturally degrade, retreating "from a state of order to disorder, [and] from complexity to simplicity."[109] But rather, in violation of the Second Law, "evolution involves a hierarchical progression to increasingly complex forms of living systems."[110] Thus, the undirected evolution from bacterium to human seems implausible at best.

Although all creatures have certain *superficial* similarities, adaptation is akin to my adding a shelf to a closet (in terms of complexity), whereas macroevolution would be more analogous to my transformation of a 100-square-foot shed into a 10,000-square-foot mansion with all the best modern amenities by *randomly* changing out one nail or piece of wood at a time—that is, without any initial planning, stopping to think about next steps, or guidance from a professional (and somehow managing to avoid getting booted out by the homeowners' association). Even though the shed and the mansion would have superficial similarities, this example points out that minor random modifications are not plausibly going to transform one into the other, nor is it credible to think that bacterium DNA might be randomly transformed into human DNA.

Biologically Possible?

Until now, we have not adequately explored the assumption by evolutionists that all changes required for an evolutionary transformation of life are *biologically possible*. Accordingly, if any necessary mutation in the chain of an evolutionary transformation were biologically impossible, then the probability that the entire transformation would take place would fall to zero. That is, if the probability of even one required link in an evolutionary chain were zero, then the probability of occurrence for the entire chain beyond that link would be zero, and evolution of the creature in question could not occur.

CONSIDER THIS

Mutations are biological *mistakes*, having no capacity to lay the groundwork for future mutations or to control where or what they change.

But are there biologically impossible macroevolutionary mutations? Scientists like Dr. Michael Behe and Dr. Stephen Meyer have given the scientific community good reason to doubt the plausibility of random, undirected mutations making wholly new, state-of-the-art organic designs. Mutations are biological *mistakes*, having no capacity to lay the groundwork for future mutations or to control where or what they change, and there are certain types of changes that blind chance cannot explain. Behe has demonstrated that many biological structures and functions cannot arise from the slow accumulation of changes, but are only functional (useful to the organism, that is) once *all* of the pieces are present.[111] Meyer, taking a different approach, has evaluated the DNA coding itself to determine whether it is reasonable to think that random mutations could create the DNA instructions required to produce new designs.[112]

Irreducible Complexity

In his book, *Darwin's Black Box*, Michael Behe describes how certain biological structures or functions are "irreducibly complex," meaning that they could not have come to be by the natural accumulation of minor changes, as demanded by evolution.[113] He provides an example of a simple mousetrap to illustrate irreducible complexity:[114] A mousetrap like the one depicted in the diagram, below, has five essential components: a platform, spring, hammer, catch and holding bar.

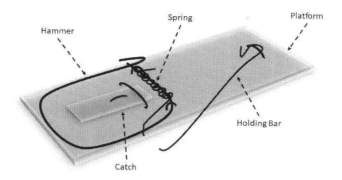

Figure 2: Mousetrap

If any of its pieces are missing, the remaining parts fail to work as a mousetrap. Even if the individual parts might have had a purpose prior to their use in a mousetrap, it still takes an intelligent agent to combine the parts for a different purpose—to catch mice.

Similarly, for the microbiological processes studied by Behe, he shows that the collection of "parts" making up their structures all have to be present to form anything purposefully functional and that the addition of the individual pieces to the organism (or cell) would serve no useful purpose prior to their coming together in complete functioning structures. Thus, there would be no known path that evolution could follow in which every change would result in improved survivability for the organism and would also ultimately construct the irreducibly complex structure and functions that Behe investigates, many of which are necessary for higher organisms to exist.

How could evolution overcome the issues raised by Behe? The cell would have to have foresight in order to re-task its components for a function or functions never previously performed. That is not easy for a designing intelligence to do (ask an engineer). Why should we have any confidence that nature could make the necessary changes *by accident*, even if it had millions of years to do it?

Complex Specified Information

Stephen Meyer has also challenged the idea that undirected, random processes of macroevolution can reasonably be expected to produce *anything* original, much less complex biological structures and functions without intelligent guidance. Even "short" DNA strands can have hundreds of thousands of base pairs, and contain *complex* information, meaning that *any* arrangement of that many items would be difficult to reproduce by chance.[115] For example, the probability of randomly duplicating a string of only 500 base pairs (about one-in-10^{301})[116] would be equivalent to winning the Mega Millions Powerball Lottery more than 35 times in a row.[117] But DNA is not merely a collection of unordered base pairs. A random sequence of base pairs is no more likely to "create" a functioning organism than a haphazard collection of computer instructions is likely to produce a useful program. DNA base pairs have a specific arrangement for the purpose of accomplishing particular functions and producing precise structures, and thereby have *specified* complexity.[118]

If DNA strands were merely random collections of base pairs, then it might be possible for mutations to transform an existing creature into something entirely different. Ironically, if everything is random and undirected, then science itself could not exist—scientists would never be able to count on the same experiment producing the same results. What reason would we have to expect, for instance, that a dog would "always" give birth to a dog of the same breed? Suppose your boss decided to call an all-hands meeting but failed to tell anyone about it and didn't establish a time, place, or purpose. It would be surprising indeed if your boss and the employees actually met together. We need information to know what is required of us at work, and all living things need specific information about what they will become and how they will function. If the information encoded in the DNA that provides that direction is random, then there could be no way of knowing what any living creature would be like. Mutations randomly modify what already exists; they do not have any knowledge of what the DNA needs to become in order to direct the creation of a new family of organisms, nor do they have the capacity to add the required information to a DNA strand (even if they did "know").[119] If Meyer is correct, then the information in a DNA strand must come from an intelligent source and macroevolution cannot be possible.

Evolution as the Creator of Life?

Evolutionists have sought to explain not only the development of all life by natural processes but also its origin—life from non-life or **abiogenesis**.[120] There surely was a period of time after the earth's beginning that it was devoid of any life. But how could life come from non-life, from the physical elements of nature that don't eat or grow or think or reproduce?

ABIOGENESIS

The inevitable inference of Darwinian evolution, that the first life must have originated from non-life

What makes something "alive"? Are we merely a collection of molecules that have luckily bound themselves together to form a bio-machine capable of reproducing, thinking, creating, transforming the earth, and exploring the universe? If so, how could that happen? Molecules have no ability to choose; they don't care about anything. Molecules do not possess a desire to find food or shelter, to procreate, or to defend themselves. On the other hand, the fittest *organisms* survive because they *want* to survive. Even plants seek nourishment to survive and grow. Molecules (and atoms) will bind with other molecules if they are close by and of the right type, but they do not go looking for other molecules to bind with, and they have no need to defend themselves against or flee from predatory molecules because there are none. How is it, then, that certain collections of molecules—those we call "organisms"—have an innate *desire* or *need* to survive? Someone might say that certain molecular combinations, the prototypes of the first organisms, survived because they randomly happened upon the nourishment or shelter that they needed. But then, we would still need an explanation for when and how those protoorganisms became *living* organisms *motivated* to survive. Moreover, we would need an explanation for how an idle cluster of molecules happened to get together with other, equally idle molecular clusters, and then organized themselves into an organism. Even the simplest of single-celled organisms is composed of an astonishingly complex system of coordinated subsystems—like miniature cities.[121] There's something fundamentally different about living things that somehow prevents scientists from being able to mix chemicals in a lab to produce life.

What *is* life? Is life no more than a collection of cooperating molecules? Are what we call "choice," "desire," "feeling," and a host of other characteristics of livings things no more than electrochemical responses to our surroundings? If so, then why do we care where we came from? Why do scientists bother to explore science? Why do we create? There is something unique about life itself that defies every evolutionary explanation. Even if it turns out that the capacity to evolve was given to the very first organisms and that we evolved from them, the essence of *life* cannot be explained or reproduced by evolution or any other natural process.

CONSIDER THIS

How could life come from non-life, from the physical elements of nature that don't eat or grow or think or reproduce?

Time to Make Room for a Creator?

The question is not whether macroevolution can be shown to be false, but whether macroevolution is a satisfactory explanation for the origin and subsequent development of all life that has ever existed. Have evolutionists made the case that life has come to be what it is *entirely apart* from the intervention or oversight of an intelligent agent?

*Micro*evolution (adaptation) *does* occur, and no one has yet proven that *micro*evolution cannot possibly result in *macro*evolution. Much remains to be demonstrated, however, before macroevolution as the creator of all living things can be viewed with the same certainty that evolution as adaptation is regarded. While macroevolution may be a legitimate scientific *hypothesis*, it has significant scientific and philosophical obstacles that it has not yet been able to overcome.

Given the shortcomings in the theory of macroevolution, it is unreasonable to deny the possibility that the origin and subsequent development of life required intelligent (divine?) intervention. I am not suggesting that scientists give up the search for a greater understanding of the natural world or that divine intervention has been proven. But

> The question is not whether macroevolution can be shown to be false, but whether macroevolution is a satisfactory explanation for the origin and subsequent development of all life that has ever existed.

insisting that evolution *must* have occurred in order to avoid the suggestion that a divine creator might have played a part in creation is not only faulty reasoning but bad science. Denying the possibility of a creator's involvement because it is not one of the answers allowed by scientific naturalism (or one's personal beliefs) is to assume the answer to the question being asked.

If we aren't even willing to *consider* a creator, then scientists seeking strictly naturalistic answers could unwittingly find themselves with no choice but to contrive scenarios that are impossible for nature to fulfill. It would be like trying to multiply 67 by 53 using a calculator that gives 999 for any answer greater than 1000, and then insisting that the correct answer has to be 999 even when the actual answer is 3551. Not only is the correct answer eliminated from consideration, but an absurd answer is left as the only viable alternative. To be fair, just as that calculator would provide correct answers for many multiplication problems (those with answers less than or equal to 999), so scientific naturalism *does* lead to reasonable explanations for many of the questions we have about nature. But there is no logical or scientific justification for assuming that naturalism can satisfactorily explain *all* there is to understand. It is time for science to make room for the possibility of a creator in the discussion of life.

Justified True Belief

There is good reason to believe that an intelligent creator exists and that he created the world and living beings. If we refuse to accept the possibility of such a creator's existence, then we cannot go wherever the evidence may lead. We would then be sacrificing reason on the altar of misguided faith, a blind insistence that physical existence and material causes are all there is and ever can be. But reason and science demand otherwise.

If there is indeed a creator, then we need to consider what that might imply. Is it reasonable to think that a creator who somehow had the wisdom to bring the orderly universe into existence did so without a purpose in mind? And if such a creator did have a purpose, is it reasonable to think his intentions for the world had nothing to do with the life that ultimately spread and filled it?[122] Are we to think he was surprised by life and, in particular, by the appearance of living beings having a rational capacity similar to his own, capable of asking questions about the nature of the world and existence itself?

The universe appears to have been designed specifically with human beings in mind. If that's the case, then there seems to be a purpose for our existence, one that a creator might be personally invested in—a purpose that we can and ought to investigate. But how are we to do this with any confidence? We're limited by the very reality in which we live. Again, unless "someone" outside of our reality tells us about our role in it, our ideas amount to no more than

---

CONSIDER THIS
The universe appears to have been designed specifically with human beings in mind.

---

individual speculation. But has he communicated to humankind his purpose in bringing the world into existence? To that question we now turn.

In Summary

- Macroevolution suffers from an "Evolution-of-the-Gaps" presumption, not unlike the "God-of-the-Gaps" explanations rejected by scientists. The "fact" of evolution is more accurately the fact of adaptation elevated to faith in an assumed conclusion.

- Macroevolution fails to provide an adequate explanation of the fossil record, which is its most important evidence for transformation of families of living things. The record lacks the expected (and necessary) transitional forms, leaving us to wonder where those thousands upon thousands of missing links might be. And contrary to what should be a gradual, haphazard evolution of various body types, the fossil record reveals a rapid, simultaneous, focused arrival on the scene of the major body plans (the Cambrian Explosion).

- Macroevolution cannot even begin to explain how evermore-complex biological organisms arose without intelligent oversight and the addition of information. Apart from the question of biological possibility, the complexity of even the simplest organisms defies explanation by random chance. Furthermore, we have good reason to question the biological plausibility of any transformation, macroevolution not having the capacity to build irreducibly complex systems nor having an adequate explanation for how existing DNA can be intelligently modified by undirected, ignorant mutations.

- Macroevolution has no explanation for the origin of life. Even if macroevolution could explain life's development once present, natural processes are wholly inadequate to grasp, much less explain, what makes something alive.

5
Made for Relationship

> "It will never be possible by pure reason
> to arrive at some absolute truth."[123]
> Werner Heisenberg, *Physics and Philosophy*

We've come a long way from where we began this journey, establishing truths about reality as well as the reality of truth, and we've also come to see that philosophical and scientific evidence point to an intelligent being as the Creator of both the world we live in and life itself on Earth. Only this Creator fits the description of "the Someone" we have wondered about, who is "outside," wholly distinct from His creation, and who would be able to give us an accurate and complete understanding of the world we inhabit. As we will discuss, He alone could tell us definitively about Himself and what His purpose is in creating this world, especially human beings. We would also expect Him to have the answers to some of the questions that concern all humanity, such as why there is evil.

While it may be reasonable to believe that the Creator of the universe knows the answers to these concerns, that does us no good unless He tells us. But what reason would He have to speak to us? That's the question we'll address in this chapter; but first, we need to understand who we are as *human* beings. What makes us different from every other created being, and why does that matter? As we explore what makes us special, we will begin to see why the Creator might want to form a relationship with us.

Uniqueness of Human Communication

Most living beings communicate in some way among their own species and even with other kinds of animals. For instance, we communicate with our pets and even have a back-and-forth dialogue of sorts. We train our dogs to respond in particular ways to our verbal and hand commands, and we hug and pet them to communicate our love for them. Dogs lick us to show affection, and they protect us from personal threats. They also communicate audibly (barking and growling), by their actions (wagging tail, licking, attacking) and by their demeanor (bared teeth). At the most basic level, all living beings communicate for their own protection, to guard their food and to defend their territory; for example, dogs growl, hummingbirds dive-bomb other hummingbirds, rattlesnakes shake their tails, bees sting, and so forth. But that's far from the whole story.

Many creatures, including beavers, ants, birds, and bees, communicate with each other according to their own "language" for the purpose of gathering food or to make, maintain, and protect their homes. For those who require a mate

> Communication seems to be *the* hallmark of intelligent life, the glue that makes familial and societal relationships possible.

to reproduce, they have various ways of attracting a partner—birds sing, show off their plumage, and even dance. And many of us have seen nature shows depicting whales and dolphins communicating via nonverbal language, that is, by sounds that other whales or dolphins understand. The importance of communication for the survival of at least some kinds of living beings cannot be overstated; ant colonies and beehives, for example, would die off if the ants and bees could not communicate with one another (ants to ants and bees to bees, that is). And lest we think that non-human life can express itself only in the interest of survival, many animals can express emotion—dogs wag their tails when happy and bear cubs cry for their mothers.[124] Whatever the method, communication seems to be one of *the* hallmarks of intelligent life, the glue that makes familial and societal relationships possible. So, as a *Divine* intelligence, we would expect communication to be a significant attribute of the Creator, but whether He would have reason or need to "converse" with us is yet to be determined.

While language is common to all animate beings, human language is exceptional, far surpassing all other animal communications in variety, complexity, content, and purpose. Not only do we have diverse language forms by which we express ourselves, but we also have a seemingly limitless ability to create new methods of communicating using those forms, such as:

- Gestures, including body language, facial expressions, and nonverbal sounds (sighs, groans, laughter, crying)

- Speech (casual conversations, lectures, sermons, discussions, debates, advertisements, songs, etc.) in any or all of the approximately 7,000 spoken languages in the world[125]

- Writing (letters, emails, texts, legal documents, poems, song lyrics, books, etc.) in any or all of the almost 4,000 written languages in the world[126]

- Art (paintings, sculptures, architecture, photographs, stained glass, tapestries)

- Music

- Dance

- Drama

- Signs and symbols (sign language, traffic signs, warning signs, religious symbols, flags, military and law enforcement insignia, etc.)

There are plenty of other examples, but the picture is clear—the human capacity to communicate is unique in the animal kingdom, entirely different from other creatures in terms of variety, extent, and complexity.

Purpose

Our communications are not just elaborate examples of whale-like nonverbal speech. If that were the case, we would have no need of words (at least, not nearly so many) to plan our day, record our history, or tell a story, nor would we have any reason (or desire) to be artistically creative. Simple sounds and body language would suffice to provide for every necessity for propagation of the human species.[127] But we do much more than merely survive.

Our language allows us to communicate complex concepts to other people, ultimately contributing to the continued growth of human communication, as we create new words and images to represent innovative ideas and then build on those, an ongoing cycle in a never-ending expansion of human language. In 2020 alone, "more than 400 new words, senses, and sub-entries [were] added to the *Oxford English Dictionary*,"[128] bringing its total word count to more than 600,000.[129] We even develop new *ways* of communicating to meet the demands of our rapidly changing culture; who would have imagined 40 years ago that we would be communicating with one another via email, text, posts on X (formerly known as Twitter), or Zoom?

Our seemingly unlimited capacity to communicate is astonishing when compared with other life forms. It would be too easy to assume that we're simply smarter animals when we focus on the similarities between us and other species, but the differences are striking and point to a human nature and design that are unlike other creatures in significant ways.[130] It begs the question: Why has the Creator designed us to be so unique, with this extravagant capacity for communication, far more than we need to merely survive?

It could be that we are merely larger-brained animals with greater control over our vocal cords and time to spend creating words upon words and forms upon forms. Is there any reason to think that we really *need* such an exceptionally flexible and dynamic capacity to communicate for more than our personal enjoyment? Perhaps our

Creator gifted us in this manner as an experiment, only to see what we would do with it, having no special purpose for us or for His creation. That seems unlikely, given the large body of evidence that the universe appears to be created with humanity in mind. At the very least, this anthropic principle—discussed previously—points to intent on the Creator's part to match our characteristics and the world He prepared.[131] Why would He do so unless He made us with a special purpose in mind, one that would require an ability to communicate so differently? To answer this question, we will need to look more closely at who we are as *human* beings.

Rational Thought

Something that may not be immediately obvious is that our superior ability to communicate is integral to human rationality, and human rationality makes it possible for us to investigate, comprehend, and live fruitfully in the natural world. We conceptualize in terms of words. Many creatures are naturally curious and explore the environment in which they live, but they do not plan their wandering about with any particular purpose in mind, except to find food or shelter. While many animals think, act, and communicate in amazing ways, they cannot conceive of (nor would they have a means of expressing) a time, place, or way of being apart from what and where they are in the current moment. Animals respond to immediate circumstances, whatever presents itself in the here and now; although they obviously have some level of memory and problem-solving capability, they do not think about yesterday, today, or tomorrow, nor can they abstractly envision "here," "there," or the distance in-between. Animals don't ever wonder if life was better in the "good ole' days" or how to offer their children a better future; nor do they imagine a better life or even life as a different species. If an image were to come into their mind (such as in a dream), they would only be able to respond to it as they would respond to the real object encountered in nature. A dog might run after a rabbit in its dream, but the dog doesn't think upon waking,

"Was that a dream, or was it real?"—or any other question that might occur to humans.[132] It's not merely that the anatomy of most animals limits their ability to verbally communicate—they simply do not have the intellectual resources to think about or express abstract ideas, ask questions, or consider any of the subtleties that distinguish human thought and communication.

Only human beings can understand that this world and all that is in it (including ourselves) exist within the context of time and space—realities we can neither escape nor control but seek to understand and work within. From our youngest days, we grow in awareness of this reality and how to live within its constraints. We begin to recognize the interconnectedness of our actions and their effects on other people, plant and animal life, and the environment, as well as how the actions of other people and our physical surroundings, in turn, affect us. The more we learn from our experiences and from others (past and present), the more we realize that the place and time we now occupy—as well as the "shape" of our own environs—have been influenced by everything that has gone before.

We are naturally able to think about *periods of time*, imagining the continuity of past moments, collectively forming the world's history. We therefore can also envision the *unfolding of time in the future*, allowing us to think ahead, to prepare, and to plan. Consequently, we communicate in *terms of duration* (minutes, hours, days, months, years, five-year plan) and the *relationship of one moment in time to another* (now, later, yesterday, today, tomorrow, two days from March 24th). Similarly, we are able to comprehend and define the *extension of individual points or locations in space* as distance, area, and volume (yards, miles, square meters, quarts), *how each location relates to another* (here, there, at your home, on Magnolia Drive, above, below, near, far), and *how individual points can be arranged* to produce various shapes (line, square, cube, box, trapezoid, hyperbola, irregular).

Our capacity to think abstractly about the natural world is what makes it possible for us to observe, define, and then employ nature's laws. We do not find the laws written down for us in some convenient "Nature for Dummies" how-to book; we discover them by observation of day-to-day events or manmade experiments and then apply them when we innovate or as we seek to explain natural occurrences. Our distinctive ability to think about this world in abstract terms is what makes it possible for us to explore and understand our universe, and to envision and create innovative technology—to accomplish whatever the human mind can conceive.

Rational Decision-Making

However simple or complex the problem, it is our ability to make *intentional* decisions through *rational* problem-solving that further distinguishes human beings from all other created beings. Whether it is deciding where to buy milk or how to build a skyscraper, we are the only species with the ability to thoughtfully determine a course of action, rationally eliminating unacceptable courses of action in order to find the best one. Even in our creative enterprises, we generally have a purpose in mind, and we rationally think through how to achieve the desired outcome.

Not only that, but human beings are at our best when we think together, exchanging and building on each other's ideas (past and present), forming communities and societies of shared knowledge—effectively extending our collaboration worldwide. We don't function like the Star Trek "Borg Collective," in which every member of the Borg thinks exactly the same thoughts as every other member. Rather, while maintaining our individuality, we can use our communication skills to work jointly in small or large communities of people, exchanging and discussing ideas, and then applying them to address the challenges we face.

So, our unique ability to communicate is at the heart of human rationality, enabling us to rationally discern and then creatively apply the laws and principles of the natural world for the flourishing of human civilization, and correspondingly for the continued growth and diversification of human communication. But why would the Creator make it possible for human beings to grow in knowledge through reasoned study and understanding of His world if He had no expectation that we would be able to do something with that knowledge? It seems an inescapable conclusion that our unique design was intentional on the part of our Creator—and if intentional, then purposeful.

Not to be too simplistic, but *it may be that we were designed with the ability to make rational choices because our Creator had important decisions for us to make.* Many of the choices we make affect the world around us in ways that the actions of other creatures do not. Unlike other species, we are not preprogrammed with limited behaviors, doing exactly what every other family member does from birth to death without questioning the purpose or wisdom of those activities. As human beings, we have the freedom to cooperate with, challenge, or even act contrary to the moral, social, and political norms of our particular community. Although human beings are not masters of nature, we don't live entirely by nature's whims, either. We cooperate with nature, but we also exercise (or attempt to exercise) governance over it—purposefully employing and forming it for whatever uses we have in mind.

CONSIDER THIS

It may be that we were designed with the ability to make rational choices because our Creator had important decisions for us to make.

Cooperation With the Creator

Sharing in our Creator's creative nature, we continuously transform the world in which we live to make life better for ourselves and others. We build businesses that provide services, products, and jobs for people; we build hospitals and veterinary clinics to care for people and animals; we care for our forests, beaches, and the environment—and much more. Even though we often disagree with one another about the methods and/or extent to which we should go to address the needs of our world, most people agree that we are not free to ignore these concerns. Certainly, the laws we make are usually intended to protect the public and our natural resources from those who would harm them.

Perhaps we act in this manner because it is in our nature to do so, that we were designed to have a special role in creation. That is not to deny that we can misunderstand what we experience, misapply what we learn, or maliciously misuse the knowledge we gain, but it is fundamental to our nature to investigate the world and then use its resources to benefit creation. On the whole, our actions demonstrate that we feel responsible to our fellow human beings and the rest of creation, yet most of us know that our actions or inactions have sometimes harmed people, animals, and nature—whether intentionally or not. The fact that *we know* that we do not always care for this world as well as we should suggests that we have an innate awareness that we are in some way responsible for it.

So, we now see that humanity's rich capacity to communicate is core to our rationality, and human reasoning plays a vital role in the decisions we make for ourselves as well as for the care of the world around us. Could it be that our Creator expected us to have *some responsibility for the administration of His creation*—learning about this world, and then rationally determining how best to use its resources for our needs and for the good of the rest of creation?

Moral Language

But where does this sense of responsibility come from? And why is it there? Most of us are aware that some of our thoughts and actions are (or have been) harmful to ourselves and others—maybe

> **CONSIDER THIS**
> Is our moral nature an accident of creation,
> or were we intentionally made to be moral creatures?

even evil. We are the only living beings that have a moral compass that distinguishes between good or bad. We have been created with a nature that innately sees them that way; we even establish laws that limit free choice according to that understanding. While there are significant differences among human societies and individuals as to what behaviors are considered good or bad, we all have an inborn sense that there are some behaviors we ought to do and others we ought not do—a conscience. While we might find some animal behaviors annoying or abhorrent, we never think of them as evil; we know that animals are governed by instinct, apart from rational moral choice. But *we* govern our behavior through a moral lens.

Our moral nature works in concert with our rational nature, *but they are not the same.* Like a governor on a car's engine that prevents a car from reaching a certain speed, our moral nature governs our actions, informing our rational thoughts, resisting actions we believe to be immoral. Since we are created with a moral nature, it should not be surprising that there are many moral values that human societies seem to universally acknowledge even if they have differing cultural values. For example, no human culture permits the indiscriminate taking of innocent human life. Societies differ as to how, by whom, and for what reasons it is or is not morally acceptable to take the life of another, but they all recognize that people are not free to kill anyone they want at any time for any reason. The same can be said of other moral principles, that cultures are constrained in some way by a shared moral sense, even if they differ on the particulars. While we don't all agree on the specifics, we all have a moral intuition that informs how we think and behave.

Societal norms and cultural values, which influence our understanding of right and wrong, cannot explain the intrinsic nature of our moral makeup. When people believe that they (or others) are being treated unfairly, they often appeal in protest to some moral principle, which suggests that we are first and foremost moral beings who are governed more by our moral intuition than by societal laws and norms. Could this sense have come from a creator who was, Himself, amoral or even immoral? No, an amoral creator wouldn't even think to create a moral being, and an immoral creator wouldn't have the capacity to make a creature with moral character that is contrary to His own character. Our moral nature must come from a creator whose nature is inherently moral and whose moral nature provides the foundation for our moral nature; we are moral beings because we have been created by a moral creator. As a moral being Himself, wouldn't He want the people He put in charge of His creation to make moral decisions?

Made for Relationship

Our Creator could have made us like other animals; instead, He made us to be rational beings with an unparalleled and extravagant capacity to communicate. Even more, He made a rational world that we—the human community—could investigate and understand so that we could shape it for the betterment of human existence. So, our Creator seems to have made us creation's caretakers and has given us a moral nature to guide our governance—but to what end, given our questionable performance? Just as it is the primary role of a parent to protect and guide children to maturity, couldn't it be that our Creator has made similar provision for us? Perhaps we were *supposed to* have a close, even intimate, ongoing relationship with Him so that we would work together as a unit—our

> Our moral nature must come from a Creator whose nature is inherently moral and whose moral nature provides the foundation for our moral nature; we are moral beings because we have been created by a moral creator.

Creator guiding us into all wisdom and imparting to us His moral desire for us to choose "the good" over personal benefit.

Love and communication are central to a strong parent-child relationship. When all goes according to design, parents first communicate their love for their children through words and demonstrations of affection and care. As children grow, words of affection and encouragement from parents (as well as words of instruction and admonishment) take on increasing importance in the growth of a loving parent-child relationship. But communication between parents and children is not one way in a healthy relationship. When children are very young, they make their thoughts and feelings known only through non-verbal communication, but as they grow older, they learn to use language to express themselves more clearly. They begin to tell their parents what they're feeling and what they want. As parents spend more time communicating with their children, the love, understanding, and trust between them grows. Would it be so hard to believe that our Creator, as an expression of His love for us, would want to communicate with us by establishing and building a relationship with us as a loving parent?

But if our Creator intends for us to have a close personal relationship with Him, how would that happen? To that question we now turn.

CONSIDER THIS

Would it be so hard to believe that our Creator, as an expression of His love for us, would want to communicate with us by establishing and building a relationship with us as a loving parent?

6
The Plausibility of "God-Speech"

Would the One who made us to seek answers to the questions that plague us, who created us with the ability to communicate in so many ways, and who made verbal interaction such an essential attribute of our nature, fail to provide a means of conversing with Him? That seems unlikely. As we conjectured in the previous chapter, our Creator displays the characteristics of a personal being, an individual—God,[133] who would want to have a relationship with the people He created.

The most amazing feature of human communication is our use of *words*—inventions of the human mind that express ideas, helping us to reason our way through the day, moment by moment. We don't merely respond to external stimuli, nor do we act strictly according to learned or instinctual behavior. So, if words, which are an expression of human thought, are so fundamental to what it means to be human, isn't it likely that words would also reflect our Creator's thought, His very nature?

But is it reasonable to think that God *would be able* to communicate with us—and we with Him? Consider the smartphone: Having the nature of a machine and a computer for its brain, the smartphone has even less in common with human beings than we have with God; and yet, I can ask Siri on my iPhone to look up something on the internet, tell "her" to take down a message and send it, call someone, or do any of a number of other tasks … and "she" does it, even verbally responding to my requests! From the smartphone's "perspective," the idea of a human being communicating with it might seem absurd, just as some people might think it impossible that God could speak with us. But from the perspective of the iPhone's creators, it's perfectly natural for us to speak to the iPhone (and it to us) because it was designed specifically to do so. So, if the creators of the iPhone can make a machine "hear" and intelligently communicate with humans, albeit limitedly, is it really all that amazing to think that our Creator could make us with the capacity to "hear" and respond to Him, in whatever form that might take? But even if it is not beyond the realm of possibility for God to speak to human beings, we need to ask whether it is plausible that God *has* spoken.

Has God Spoken?

Many people disregard the possibility of God-speech[134] for a variety of reasons:

- They do not believe God exists (atheism).
- They believe God has no particular interest in the world He created (deism).
- They believe in multiple "gods" that have power or authority over various aspects of human existence but don't communicate their wishes to us or care about our requests (polytheism).

Other people believe in something godlike but impersonal—neither a creator nor a communicator like "The Force" of Star Wars that somehow influences life on Earth. In fact, it's not unusual to hear someone say something like, "I put 'it' out to the universe," as if the universe has the capacity to listen and respond; yet many of those same people would deny the possibility that God could actually hear us and act on our behalf.

The Plausibility of "God-Speech"

Nevertheless, most people in the world (approximately 55% according to Pew Research)[135] profess Judeo-Christian or Muslim religious affiliation, religions that teach the existence of God as the Creator and Supreme Being who *has* "spoken" to His creatures over the millennia. That doesn't mean that all who profess these religious affiliations necessarily believe everything their religion teaches, but it suggests that much of the world has some belief that God speaks and also listens to our requests (what most people call "prayer"). So, who is right about the reality of God-speech?

While it would be impossible to prove the negative (that God has *never* spoken to anyone at any time throughout history), some people offer as evidence against God-speech that "He has never spoken *to me*." Of course, the implication is that if God has not spoken to them, then He hasn't spoken to anyone else, either. But that is quite a leap. The President, for instance, has never spoken *to me*, but we know that he speaks to the American people and often to the world at large, both audibly and in writing. Usually, I am made aware of his messages through the news media or others who tell me what he's said, but he doesn't have to speak to me directly for me to know that he *has* spoken and for me to be aware of his message. In like manner, God might have spoken in the past to humankind through one or more intermediaries or messengers without speaking to every person individually.

Our thinking or behavior could also affect how (or whether) we hear and receive God's messages. For example, if I don't like the President or don't believe he has any authority to speak into my life, I might ignore or intentionally reject whatever he has to say. And even if I do think that I should pay attention to him, I might still reject what he says because I disagree with his position or simply because I don't like its implications for me. There may be additional reasons that we fail to pay heed to what God has said that have nothing

> God might have spoken in the past to humankind through one or more intermediaries or messengers without speaking to every person individually.

to do with whether or not He has actually spoken (whether verbally or in writing). Some people refuse to give ear to what are plausibly God's communications because they blame Him for the suffering in the world, or they don't believe He exists. Even people who have no reason to shut out or ignore God-speech may have trouble "hearing" Him because of the many distractions in their lives. Returning to the iPhone example, Siri doesn't get everything 100% right. If I tried to talk to "her" in a noisy car or room, she wouldn't be able to fully distinguish my words from the background noise—nor would I be able to hear "her" clearly. Could it be that life's distractions—the noise in our lives—might have a similar effect on our ability to hear from God?

To determine whether God has spoken, we'll need criteria that are more verifiable than what we can determine solely from personal experiences; we will need markers that point not only to the plausibility of God-speech but also to its likelihood. We're interested in an explanation of this world that can be trusted as authoritative, one that we can rely on to answer our questions. If God has truly spoken, it seems logical to expect that His communications would have certain characteristics. But what would they be?

Expectations of God-Speech

In order to evaluate whether alleged instances of God-speech are more plausibly true than not, we will need to think about the kinds of evidence we would expect to find in support of those claims. This is not a complete evaluation. The criteria I have identified below may be biased toward my own beliefs, but while the satisfaction of all these conditions cannot be counted as proof positive that God has spoken, I have attempted to identify several tests an honest evaluator would require of any such claim.

1. Proper Credentials

In general, the people we listen to are those we accept as having authority or expertise. They might include parents, teachers, bosses, medical professionals, police, fire fighters, journalists, authors, religious figures, and others. Authority figures first establish their position of leadership before giving directions that others are expected to follow. For instance, we don't respond in the same way to a civilian who gives us an order as we do to the police. Consequently, law enforcement officials wear identifying clothing, announce themselves, and show their badges, all of which confirm their right to act in a position of authority. Likewise, we should expect God to establish His authority when He speaks. Identifying Himself as God would certainly be one way, but we might also expect His authority to be established by *what happens when He speaks.* For example, someone who is unfamiliar with American police uniforms would still recognize the authority of an officer upon seeing that person redirect traffic. They would know that police officers have true authority by observing what happens (or stops happening) when they speak: People stop and listen, traffic stops or changes direction, and people do as they are told (most of the time). We should expect to find similar evidence of God's authority by His interactions with the world and with people. People respond to a law officer performing job-specific duties; similarly, people "tuned in" to recognizing God's actions react/obey accordingly.

"God" is the English word we use to refer in a general sense to one or more Divine beings, just as "person" or "people" are the English words we use to refer to one or more human beings. But we don't call each other "person"; we have names that help us distinguish one person from another. Our names are special to us, even if we're not named after someone particular, and even if many people have the same name. We still recognize our name as *ours*, and we like having people say it (except, as a child, when we've done something wrong). So, we might infer that God, the One who created the universe, has a name by which He would want to be called, one that is uniquely His. We would expect Him to tell us His name.

However, even a name is not sufficient to identify one individual to the exclusion of all others; many people have the exact same name as someone else. When someone says to us, for example, "Do you know Jim Smith?" we typically respond by saying something along the lines of: "You mean the Jim Smith who works at Starbucks?" or "The Jim Smith with red hair?" or "The one with a great sense of humor?" We distinguish people who have the same name by what they do, how they look, how they behave, where they live, who they are related to, and other personal traits that narrow the possibilities down to only one person. The same is true of God. So, if God wants us to know when *He* is speaking and not another "god," we will also need to know which characteristics are specific to His Divine personhood. To verify that a communication is from *the* God and no other so-called god(s), we'll need to know what characteristics are uniquely embodied by God—specific to His nature and activity on behalf of the world.

For example, we know that *the* God is the One who created the universe. As we've seen in previous chapters, a god who is not separate from the universe could not be the Creator God, nor could an impersonal being. We would expect God's unique characteristics to be found in communications acknowledged to be from Him, and we would expect His actions to be consistent with those characteristics, including those things we already believe to be true about Him. We should be very skeptical if we hear from someone claiming to speak as God or His envoy, but whose message is self-contradictory or inconsistent with reality as we've come to know it.

We would also assume that any communication claiming to contain God-speech would plainly record or quote what God (or His preferred name) said directly or what He said through an intermediary. Otherwise, why would we bother to consider the writer's claim of God-speech? The person's words might contain truth, but we're not seeking just any truth. I believe that what I have written in this book is true, but I am making no claim to be writing words received directly from God. We want to know what "the Someone" who brought this world and us into existence—the Creator God—has to say.

2. Intimate Knowledge of Human Nature

We have seen that it is more plausible than not that God exists and that He created the universe and us, and even that He finely tuned the universe, especially planet Earth, just for human habitation. More than that, if God's purpose in creating the universe was to make a place for us to live, then He likely had a purpose for creating us. If so, then we would expect God to tell us why we have been so honored, why we are so special to Him. In particular, we'd want to know if we were created for an intimate relationship with Him. We'd also want to know if God expects anything of us and whether or not we have some eternal purpose and destiny. Otherwise, why would we care if God has spoken?

As we have discussed, *all* human beings believe that there is a right way to live; what differs among us is what we believe that right way is. Is our moral nature an accident of creation, or were we intentionally made to be moral creatures? As our Creator, God should have something to say about that, telling us whether there is an all-encompassing morality and, if so, what the consequences and rewards are for adhering to, or violating, that morality.

3. Rationally Truthful

Since God is the only "Someone" who can tell us accurately about our world, a primary characteristic of God-speech would be truthfulness. His "messages" to us should both correspond to what we think we know about the world and human nature and also reveal what we wouldn't otherwise know. Furthermore, God-speech should be consistent within a communication, and multiple messages believed to be from God must be consistent with each other in what they teach.

> Since God is the only "Someone" who can tell us accurately about our world, a primary characteristic of God-speech would be truthfulness.

4. Accommodated to Humanity

It should not be surprising to find that God has accommodated our limited ability to understand, especially since He is an eternal Being communicating with finite beings who are gradually learning about the world He created. Therefore, it would be sensible to discover that His messages have changed in depth of insight as humankind learned from Him and grew in its capacity to understand and respond, just as parents speak in a manner that accommodates their child's level of development. Newer messages would build on the foundation laid by previous ones without contradicting them.

5. Historical Evidence

God's spoken word should be trustworthy in its record of history, culture, and geography. We should expect that God would ensure that His recorded words would be thoroughly honest with regard to the information they include about people, places, events, and all other details that set the background for His communications or interactions with humanity.

More to the point, if the Creator of the universe has truly spoken, then we should expect His words to have some effect on the lives of people and societies over all time—how we understand our place and purpose in the world. God's words might challenge how we live and act toward one another in ways that conflict with our selfish desires. Just as adults view the world and understand right behavior in ways that young children cannot, we would expect the Creator of the universe to be much wiser than us and to guide us into that wisdom.

In addition to His wisdom, it would not be surprising if God's spoken word has led to "supernatural" events on Earth that override nature's normal functioning. Evidence of such occurrences could help identify certain communications as the work of Divinity or a divinely empowered spokesperson; such accompanying supernatural events could give Divine authority to words claimed to be spoken by God or in His name.

A God who is eternal and "outside" the constraints of time may also speak prophetically of future events to, and through, the people He created. Prophetic messages from God might contain warnings or promises; this should be expected if God created human beings with a plan and purpose, demonstrating His dominion over all human affairs. We should not be surprised to find prophetic words fulfilled in history, validating them as originating with the only true God.

God-Speech Candidate

> **CONSIDER THIS**
> Do we expect the Creator of the universe to be much wiser than us and to guide us into that wisdom?

Armed with a way to evaluate claims of God-speech, we can now ask whether any communication claimed to be from God (or, more generally, from a Divine source) has some or all of the above marks of Divine authorship. Having applied these criteria to many documents over the years, I have found the Bible—comprised of the Hebrew Scriptures and the New Testament—to be the singular document that seems to fit the necessary characteristics of God-speech, that plausibly fulfills those criteria (see Appendix C: Evaluation Criteria and the Bible for evidence of God-speech in the Bible).

In the following chapters, we will consider what God has told us in the Bible regarding the questions that plague humanity.

7
First Words

In the previous chapter, we discovered that a primary purpose for
our extravagant gift of communication and human rationality is to
communicate with God—and He with us (God-speech). Having
established its plausibility, we then considered the characteristics of
God-speech that we would expect to encounter in any writing
claiming to be a communication from God, and we concluded that
the Bible is one such document.

In this chapter, then, we will examine a representative sampling
of writings from the Bible to learn what it claims that God has said
about His purpose in creating this world and, especially, human
beings. Then, of course, we will want to know what that means for
you and for me.

Introduction to the Bible

Many people believe the Bible to be the definitive collection of
God's communications to humankind. It is a compilation of 66
"books"[136] divided into two major and distinct but corresponding
accounts of God's creation and His subsequent interactions with that
world. The first division is referred to as the "Hebrew Scriptures," or
"Old Testament," and is comprised of 39 books written between
1500 and 400 BC.[137] The second is referred to as the "New
Testament," and is comprised of 27 books written in the latter half of

the first century AD,[138] some of which are eyewitness accounts of the life of Jesus, the Son of God, and of the fulfillment of God's promises as documented in the Hebrew Scriptures. Other New Testament writings provide further insight into the importance of these events for humankind.

But what is a "testament," and why the *New* Testament? "Testament" comes from the Latin for a "will" (as in "God's will") and translates a Greek word meaning "covenant," which is an agreement or contract between two or more parties. As recorded in the Bible, God's contracts with humankind are distinctive in that God, having no equal in power and authority, establishes them without needing or seeking human acceptance of His conditions or stipulations—but with corresponding benefits for complying and penalties for disobeying. He chooses certain people to enter into a special relationship with Him, in which He commits Himself to the requirements of His covenant and calls on those He has chosen to commit to those requirements as well so that they may partake of His promised blessings.[139] As the name suggests, then, the *New* Testament tells us of a new covenant between God and humankind, and that implies that there was an earlier covenant that had been in effect, a covenant that is documented in the Hebrew Scriptures, or more descriptively, the "Old" Testament.

The earlier covenant was God's contract with the ancient Israelites, the ancestors of the Jewish people, many of whom live in the modern nation of Israel.[140] The acts of God leading to the establishment of that covenant and its subsequent unfolding in the history of ancient Israel are detailed in the Hebrew Scriptures.[141] The Hebrew Scriptures testify to creation, the rebellion of humans against God, the initiation of a first covenant with Israel, Israel's failure to be faithful to that covenant, and promises of the ultimate restoration of humankind's relationship with God. The New Testament records the beginning of the fulfillment of God's promises, in which God reveals how *all people*—not only the Israelites—may be restored to a right relationship with Him through belief in Jesus Christ.

But what exactly does the Bible have to say, and why should we believe that it faithfully records God's interactions with humankind, that it is a record of God-speech? To answer that question, we will begin at the beginning, with Genesis, the first book of the Bible.

The Beginning (Genesis 1:1)

Although it wasn't written until about 1500 BC,[142] the first book of the Bible, Genesis, opens with the creation of the world and answers some of the questions that concern humankind:

- where the world came from
- the origin of plant, animal, and human life
- something about human nature, including God's purpose for creating human beings

The very first words of Genesis are: "In the beginning, God created the heavens and the earth."[143] While our English word "god" has an ambiguous meaning, generally referring to a Divine being or presence but not positively identifying any particular entity, we know that the God of Genesis 1:1 cannot be just any god; He is uniquely identified as the One (*the only One*) who created everything that exists.

The Hebrew word for "created" (*bara'*) is used to describe "the divine activity of fashioning something new, fresh and perfect."[144] The verse doesn't necessarily mean that God created the universe from nothing (*ex nihilo*); He could have formed the universe as something completely new, from existing material. But even if God formed the universe from existing material, we would still have to ask where that material came from. Recalling Leibniz's argument for God in Chapter 3, the material of the universe does not exist apart from the creative work of God bringing it into being. So, we would expect that Genesis would tell us that God created the material first and then formed it into the universe or brought all material and the form of the universe into being in one or more Divine acts.[145]

103

These first words of Genesis also assume that God was already present prior to "the beginning." He did not come into being along with His creation; if that were the case, then someone or something would have had to create Him, and that would lead to the absurdity of a never-ending series of "creators." Rather, He was (and is) an entirely distinct or separate Being outside of creation. This God is nothing like the god of pantheism, a god that is somehow identical to the universe, because the God of the Bible exists independently from the universe. Additionally, since "In the beginning..." does not refer to *God's* beginning but to the point at which the universe began to exist, that suggests a beginning of time as well.[146] Just as a stopwatch isn't started in a race until the gun goes off, Genesis 1:1 implies that our human measure of past, present, and future began with the creation of the universe.

But why should we believe that Genesis 1:1 was given to us by God, that the words are anything more than the musings of some ancient human being? The simple, straightforward statement of Genesis 1:1 was profound when it was first written and is even more so now, given our 21st century understanding of the formation of the universe. It was not until Einstein's General Theory of Relativity and Hubble's study of the Galactic Redshift together produced convincing evidence in the early 20th century that we had scientific reasons to believe that the universe had a beginning, that biblical beliefs about the creation of the world became grounded in something other than faith and philosophical argumentation.[147] And yet, some 3,500 years ago, a group of people who were ignorant of what we would call modern science held this truth as foundational to their convictions. There are many other ancient stories of creation, of course, but none of them come close to the specific truth revealed by those first words in the Genesis account of the origin of the world.[148]

Is it possible that the writer of Genesis just made it up, or was re-counting a cultural story? Maybe, but is it likely? It would be almost 3500 years before anyone—other than those who believed the

Genesis account—would acknowledge that the world may have been created. And for good reason. We all experience time as a continuum of one second melting into another and physical reality as ever-changing but having such an enormousness and permanence that it's hard to imagine there could ever have been a time when it didn't exist. How could it be that scientifically ignorant people knew what only the most recent scientific discoveries have revealed? The explanation that I think is compelling is that God actually *revealed* these truths about the universe, time, and Himself to those who recorded them in Genesis.

In summary, Genesis 1:1 states or implies:

1. God did not have a beginning; He always existed.

2. "God" refers to *the* supreme Being who has authority over His creation and everything in it.

3. The universe had a beginning. God created the universe from nothing, either by creating the material first and then fashioning it, or by creating the universe in one or more Divine acts.

4. God is separate from His creation.

5. Time had a beginning. God initiated time as we understand and experience it when He created the universe.

6. God is not constrained by time; that is, He is eternal.

7. God revealed these truths to human beings; consequently, Genesis 1:1 is likely the first biblical account of God-speech.

Days of Creation (Gen. 1:2–2:3)

Genesis 1:1 is a summary statement about God's creation of the "heavens and the earth," and what follows are some of the details known as "the days of creation." Beginning with Genesis 1:2, we find ourselves on an Earth that has already been created but is featureless (formless), devoid of pretty much everything and without the light that is essential to life:

² The earth was without form and void, and darkness was over the face of the deep. And the Spirit of God was hovering over the face of the waters.

In the ensuing verses, the earth's surface is formed, filled, and bathed with heavenly light(s) according to God's spoken word (God-speech), which brings forth all physical realities and living beings:

³ And God said, "Let there be light," and there was light. …
⁶ And God said, "Let there be a vault between the waters to separate water from water." ⁷ So God made the vault and separated the water under the vault from the water above it. And it was so. ⁸ God called the vault "sky."
⁹ And God said, "Let the water under the sky be gathered to one place, and let dry ground appear." And it was so. …
¹¹ Then God said, "Let the land produce vegetation: seed-bearing plants and trees on the land that bear fruit with seed in it, according to their various kinds." And it was so. …
¹⁴ And God said, "Let there be lights in the vault of the sky to separate the day from the night and let them serve as signs to mark sacred times, and days and years, ¹⁵ and let them be lights in the vault of the sky to give light on the earth." And it was so. …
²⁰ And God said, "Let the water teem with living creatures, and let birds fly above the earth across the vault of the sky." ²¹ So God created the great creatures of the sea and every living thing with which the water teems and that moves about in it, according to their kinds, and every winged bird according to its kind. …
²⁴ And God said, "Let the land produce living creatures according to their kinds: the livestock, the creatures that move along the ground, and the wild animals, each according to its kind." And it was so. …
²⁶ Then God said, "Let us make mankind in our image, in our likeness, so that they may rule over the fish in the sea and the birds in the sky, over the livestock and all the wild animals, and over all the creatures that move along the ground." ²⁷ So God created mankind in His own image, in the image of God He created them; male and female He created them.

Notice how matter-of-factly God's actions are stated. Unlike pagan deities throughout history—who act like out-of-control men and women with super*human* powers[149]—the God of Genesis has the power to accomplish exactly what He intends in a rational manner, regardless of the actions of any other being. God merely commands, and His spoken word brings the universe and all living things into existence.

CONSIDER THIS

Unlike pagan deities throughout history—who act like out-of-control men and women with super*human* powers—the God of Genesis has the power to accomplish exactly what He intends in a rational manner, regardless of the actions of any other being.

Having created all life by His spoken word, God then speaks *directly to* some of the creatures He created, commanding them to be fruitful, to fill their respective habitats, and to eat the food prepared for them:

> [22] God blessed [the water creatures and birds] and said, "Be fruitful and increase in number and fill the water in the seas, and let the birds increase on the earth." ...
> [28] God blessed [mankind] and said to them, "Be fruitful and increase in number; fill the earth and subdue it. Rule over the fish in the sea and the birds in the sky and over every living creature that moves on the ground."
> [29] Then God said, "I give you every seed-bearing plant on the face of the whole earth and every tree that has fruit with seed in it. They will be yours for food.
> [30] And to all the beasts of the earth and all the birds in the sky and all the creatures that move along the ground—everything that has the breath of life in it—I give every green plant for food." And it was so.

But God says more to humankind, giving us dominion over all other creatures and over the earth.[150] As we previously speculated, it does seem that God intends for us to act as His stewards over all living things and to "subdue the earth," that is, to use it for our purposes, preserving His creation.

God gave humanity authority to govern all living things on His behalf and even to mold creation to our particular needs. That does not mean that we were given license to harm God's creation, to abuse Earth's resources in whatever way we choose. God declared every part of His creation to be "good" and His collective works to be "very good;"[151] so, He would not turn creation over to us to exploit it for our own selfish purposes. The idea is that we would act in God's place in the administration of His creation, treating all forms of life with the same care that He has for them. We get some sense of this in Genesis 2:18-20, where Adam is given the responsibility of naming all other living beings, suggesting a respectful bond between humans and animals. So, to be made in God's image and likeness is, at least in part, to share in God's authority and responsibility over the created order. We are to echo His creative nature and "subdue" creation, molding or forming it for *good (beneficial)* purposes. This explains why God gave humans such an incredible capacity to think rationally and communicate with one another as well as with Him.

The many physical similarities between all living things with respect to form, function, and genetic makeup seem to suggest a common designer, just as the bold brush strokes of the paintings *Starry Night* and *Irises* point to their creator, Vincent van Gogh. As the common

> To be made in God's image and likeness is, at least in part, to share in God's authority and responsibility over the created order.

characteristics of the paintings tell us about van Gogh's artistic technique and personality, so the shared attributes among living things reveal part of God's personality, His creative diversity, and His engineering prowess. But God did something different, something extraordinary, when it came to human beings, intentionally revealing something of Himself through *us*. Genesis 1:26 tells us that God made human beings uniquely, *in His own image and likeness*. That does not mean that we were made to look like God in some physical sense; God is a non-physical (immaterial) spirit who has a nature wholly distinct from our own. And yet, He declared that we were made in His image and likeness, implying that the uniqueness of our reasoning as well as our creative and moral capacities are reflections of God's own nature. Could it also be that God made us to have something of His spiritual nature as well? We'll look at this question in the discussion of Genesis 2:4-25, where we are given more details about the creation of the first human beings.

Why should we believe that the biblical account is truthful, that God created all living beings just by speaking? When examined closely, the biblical creation account has little in common with the creation, "fall," and flood stories[152] of ancient mythologies. For instance, contrasting the Genesis account with the "Epic of Gilgamesh," an epic poem from ancient Mesopotamia, the Genesis account is told as narrative history of God's commands and subsequent results, while the "Epic of Gilgamesh" has the characteristics of a legend, as can be seen from the following excerpt: "So the goddess conceived an image in her mind, and … She dipped her hands in water and pinched off clay, she let it fall in the wilderness, and noble Enkidu was created."[153] While Genesis certainly asks us to accept some concepts that are beyond our everyday experiences of reality, the depiction of how creation took place is not irrational, and the narrative has none of the characteristics of a fanciful story. Rather, it's a sober report, told like we might expect of a reporter who had interviewed eyewitnesses. The seriousness of the creation account certainly does not prove its truthfulness, but its report-like genre sets it apart as a genuine attempt to convey truth.

> Why should we believe that the biblical account is truthful, that God created all living beings just by speaking?

One of the markers that sets Genesis apart as a direct statement of truth is its counting of the days of creation, beginning in Genesis 1:5 with, "And there was evening, and there was morning—the first day." Days Two through Six are counted according to the same pattern. The identification and numbering of each day suggests that God was in complete control, directing His creation in an orderly, methodical manner, one aspect of creation at a time.[154]

Nothing God created was unintended or unexpected. God created every element of nature and every *kind* ("family" in our modern scientific understanding) of creature that has ever existed, as well as the means for each of its kind to diversify and fill the earth. As previously discussed, we know that there are natural physical laws that govern the motion of the celestial bodies, we know that there are natural biological laws that govern how living things adapt, and we know that those laws do not exist by themselves. In fact, they're not laws at all in the sense of being inviolable principles of existence that could never have been otherwise. Rather, what we call "natural laws" are really *human* observations of the way nature is, *not what caused it to be that way*. Our observations tell us nothing about *why* anything exists but, rather, are characteristics of that which God has made to exist. When God created the physical universe, He imbued it with the laws that govern its existence and characteristics. Gravity, for instance, acts only where there is something with mass to cause it to act; a "Law of Gravity" doesn't exist apart from some physical object that produces the effect we call "gravity." Similarly, the laws governing life, such as the process of deoxyribonucleic acid (DNA) replication, are meaningless until there is life to govern. The creation of the universe and of life cannot be separated from the creation of the natural laws that govern their existence.

CONSIDER THIS
What we call "natural laws" are really *human* observations of the way nature is, *not what caused it to be that way.*

God planned certain kinds or families of creatures to be brought forth, but He also provided for the numerous *varieties* that arose from those "kinds" to develop through the action of natural adaptation. Beagles, greyhounds, and collies, for example, are instances of the variations that have developed in the dog family.[155] There is no reason to think that God was surprised by the diversity that resulted. In other words, God knew exactly what He was doing and *why* He was doing it; He had a *purpose* for every facet of the created order. Even where we are not specifically given the purpose in the creation account, we can see that there is intent in the detailed ordering and description of creation; nothing was done haphazardly. The creation account is incompatible with macroevolution as a means of life's development because evolution specifically denies the necessity or involvement of God in the formation of life, while Genesis clearly states the opposite. According to Genesis, nothing happened in creation (or subsequent to creation) apart from God's oversight and direction. Consequently, nothing came to be in creation that God did not plan *or* foresee, either through His direct creation or through the mechanisms of the natural physical and biological laws that He also created.

The author of Genesis 1 wrote as if he had been given a ringside seat to the act of creation. Of course, that cannot be literally true because no human being existed at the beginning of creation; so either the account was imagined, or the events of creation were revealed to the author by the only one with the detailed knowledge of what transpired—God.[156] We have good reason to believe the latter, given our modern understanding of the world's development. Genesis 1:1 documented the beginning of the universe and of time (in human-defined terms) at least 3500 years before modern science "discovered" these truths. And the statements of Genesis 1:2-24 are no less astounding for their pre-scientific accuracy, finding substantial agreement with modern science.[157] The fact that there is any agreement should make us wonder how the author of Genesis could have come to such a clear conception of the world's creation by pure speculation, especially when other ancient sources are so muddled, filled with superstitious stories.

While the Bible doesn't provide the kinds of explanations we'd find in a science textbook, that doesn't mean that scientists should disregard its claims. If God created, then there must be a point at which natural processes had a beginning. Prior to that moment, natural processes wouldn't have existed, so theories about the origins of the physical world that ignore God's creative work will have explanatory gaps or questionable hypotheses where the existing evidence exposes discontinuities from one stage of development to another (or from nonexistence to existence). Such jumps are not what would be expected of continuous natural processes.[158]

Beyond the various details of God's creative works, He also tells us in Genesis what He thinks of the results, calling the major works of creation "good." Then, after the creation of human beings in verse 27, God reviews creation as a whole and declares it to be "very good" in verse 31. Nothing God created is lacking in goodness.

Summarizing the claims and implications of God's creative works according to Genesis 1:2-2:3:

1. God speaks creation into existence. God's spoken words of command were alone sufficient to bring all physical reality and life into being.

2. God speaks to the living things He has created, suggesting that they are capable of receiving and obeying His commands. God speaks to human beings like He speaks to the other creatures, clearly expecting us to be able to receive His communications and act in accordance with them.[159]

3. Human beings are made in God's image and likeness, to be representative of God's character and qualities, including our reasoning, creative, and moral capacities. God appoints humankind to rule over all living creatures and to subdue the earth for our purposes. This role suggests the need for a sophisticated level of human understanding as well as the need for cooperation between God and humanity, even two-way communication.

4. The creation account is a sober, rational report, completely unlike ancient mythologies. There is nothing about it that comes across as contrived but, rather, as a genuine effort to report truth.

5. The identification and numbering of each day suggests that God was in complete control, directing His creation in an orderly, methodical manner, one act of creation at a time.

6. Nothing God created was unintended or unexpected; rather, He had (or has) a purpose for every facet of the created order.

7. The Bible may not provide the kinds of explanations we would expect to find in a science textbook, but the details provided by the Genesis creation account are critical for properly understanding the formation and development of life.

8. All that God creates is "good," and God considers His whole act of creation to be "very good." As every part of God's creation is "good," so human beings were created "good"— having the essence of goodness as a creature of God. As we will see, that doesn't mean that we remained morally good.

But if God created every part of the physical world and it is all "good," where do illness, physical deformities, and natural disasters come from? And what about the various plants and creatures that can harm human beings, or people who treat other people badly? We will address this important question when we look at Genesis chapters 2 and 3, accounts that focus on the creation of the first human beings and their disastrous failure at following and obeying their Creator right from the start.

8
Humanity's Failure

Humanity Corrupted (Genesis 2:4–3:7)

So, why does the creation narrative seem to contradict much of what we know about the world in which we live? There are many ways in which human beings exploit this creation—its material and animal resources—as well as other people. With natural disasters, illnesses, diseases, dangerous creatures, poisonous plants, and the harm people inflict on one another, the original order and peace of creation is not our daily experience. According to Genesis 1:29-30, people were made to eat plants and fruit rather than other living creatures. But suffering and death are everywhere. If the author of Genesis is correct, then something has clearly changed. How then are we to make sense of the obvious inconsistencies between the biblical account and our experience?

We need to read a bit further into Genesis to find clues to the answer. Genesis 2:4 begins a second account of creation, focusing our attention on the first human being:

> 4 This is the account of the heavens and the earth when they were created, when the LORD God made the earth and the heavens.
> 5 Now no shrub had yet appeared on the earth and no plant had yet sprung up, for the LORD God had not sent rain on the earth and there was no one to work the ground, 6 but streams came up from the earth and watered the whole surface of the ground. 7 Then the

> LORD God formed a man from the dust of the ground and breathed into his nostrils the breath of life, and the man became a living being.
> 8 Now the LORD God had planted a garden in the east, in Eden; and there he put the man he had formed.

The first thing to notice is that "LORD" is the uniquely personal name of God,[160] which He gives because God's relationship with humanity is different than with any other created beings; with people, it's *personal*. Even though the first human is made from "the dust of the ground" (natural elements) as with God's other creatures, God breathes His spirit into the man to make him a living being. As a being animated by God's spirit, we begin to understand what it must mean for Adam (the Hebrew word for "man") to be made in God's image and likeness.

Next, we are introduced to the Garden of Eden, which had already been created just for Adam. The Garden had many fruit-bearing trees that were made for his pleasure and to satisfy his hunger, two of which were special—the tree of life and the tree of the knowledge of good and evil.[161] And God gave Adam responsibility and a command:

> 15 The LORD God took the man and put him in the Garden of Eden to work it and take care of it. 16 And the LORD God commanded the man, "You are free to eat from any tree in the garden; 17 but you must not eat from the tree of the knowledge of good and evil, for when you eat from it you will certainly die."

From the beginning, God had a close, personal relationship with Adam. This command is the first clear instance of God speaking directly to Adam, and God gave Adam the responsibility of caring for the Garden that had been specially prepared for him. Adam's freedom, however, was not unrestricted; God commanded him not to eat of the tree of the knowledge of good and evil because it would lead to his death. But what did that mean to Adam? We don't know if Adam had ever seen death, but even if he had, it's unlikely that he fully appreciated the significance of God's warning.[162] In any event, he had only one rule to follow; God had made life simple for Adam. His work was not arduous labor but gave him purpose. Most people who have lived long enough know that the retirement dream of kicking back and doing nothing does not really make us happy—at least not for long. We all need to be actively engaged in living and have a reason to get up in the morning.

Adam, however, had none of the woes and worries that we all have to contend with; he was living the idyllic life … with one exception: Adam had no suitable companionship.

> [18] The LORD God said, "It is not good for the man to be alone. I will make a helper suitable for him."
> [19] Now the LORD God had formed out of the ground all the wild animals and all the birds in the sky. He brought them to the man to see what he would name them; and whatever the man called each living creature, that was its name. [20] So the man gave names to all the livestock, the birds in the sky and all the wild animals. But for Adam no suitable helper was found. [21] So the LORD God caused the man to fall into a deep sleep; and while he was sleeping, he took one of the man's ribs and then closed up the place with flesh. [22] Then the LORD God made a woman from the rib he had taken out of the man, and he brought her to the man.
> [23] The man said, "This is now bone of my bones and flesh of my flesh; she shall be called 'woman,' for she was taken out of man."
> [24] That is why a man leaves his father and mother and is united to his wife, and they become one flesh. [25] Adam and his wife were both naked, and they felt no shame.

Even if some people do not take this account of the woman's (Eve) creation literally, the clear intent is that Eve's nature was to be the same as Adam's and that Eve was to be special to Adam as his perfect companion. This is consistent with the first creation account in which it is clear (according to Genesis 1:27b) that Eve was also made in the image of God. And though Eve was taken from Adam, making two, they were to become one again through the intimacy of marriage. Adam and Eve were made for a trusting relationship with each other, which flowed from a trusting relationship with God. They had no sense of shame or humiliation regarding their nakedness—of body or inner person—either between themselves or before God. They were wholly innocent, having no secrets.

Then something terrible happened in that pristine Garden. In Genesis 3, a different kind of creature arrives on the scene. He is called "the serpent" because of the form in which he appears, while other portions of the Bible identify him as "Satan" or "the devil."[163] As the adversary of humankind—for that is what his names mean— Satan seeks to trick Eve (and through her, Adam) into eating from the tree of the knowledge of good and evil. The serpent knows that they will die, and he believes that God's purposes for humanity will consequently be thwarted.[164]

Satan succeeds in part, first in planting a seed of questioning in Eve's mind, encouraging her to wonder whether there's a way to get around God's command, asking, "Did God actually say…?"[165] Then, he challenges God's goodness, suggesting that God is withholding something good from her and Adam, saying, "You will not certainly die … For God knows that when you eat from [the tree] your eyes will be opened, and you will be like God, knowing good and evil."[166] According to Satan, then, God is lying about the threat of death *and* He is withholding from Adam and Eve a much better life in which they would be free to fulfill their every desire, deciding for themselves what is good and what is not. What happens next isn't hard to guess: "When [Eve] saw that the fruit of the tree was good for food and pleasing to the eye, and also desirable for gaining wisdom, she took some and ate it. She also gave some to her husband, who was with her, and he ate it."[167]

Evil had officially entered God's good world.

The Problem of Evil

God could have made the world a horrible place to live in, with us as His menial slaves, but instead, God made it the perfect place for human habitation. He made us in His own image and likeness, with a rational and moral nature like His own and with awesome authority and responsibility over creation. God didn't need to create us, but He made us in His goodness, for relationship with Him and to share in the bounty of His creation. "The good" doesn't change according to human determinations, accommodating our personal or societal preferences, but is always in accordance with God's good nature. Consequently, evil is whatever departs from God's good.

But how does evil arise in God's good creation?

Among other attributes, human beings have a rational and moral nature. While our choices are occasionally driven by instinct (for example, when we are afraid), we have the capacity to think through

> God didn't need to create us, but He made us in His goodness, for relationship with Him and to share in the bounty of His creation.

problems and make difficult decisions, decisions that are often influenced by our moral intuition, what we believe to be "the good." All other creatures do what they do mostly by instinct, apart from a rational thought process and devoid of moral considerations. While we might be repulsed by the thought of being attacked by a dog—or any animal for that matter—we don't assume that the animal intends evil when it attacks; we know that it is only acting in accordance with its nature, not stopping to consider whether it is violating some moral law.

Of course, animals sometimes perform amazing feats to protect their owners—and they no doubt receive approval for their actions—but our pets don't do those things out of a sense of moral obligation, choosing a higher good over the possible consequences to themselves. While we may be thankful for their protection, we don't think of our pets as *morally pure* nor, by contrast, do we ever think of charging cats with mouse murder. We do, however, hold owners morally accountable for their dogs' actions if they fail to protect innocent people from unprovoked attacks. We have moral obligations and have been given the capacity to make moral decisions that affect not only our own well-being, but as stewards of God's creation, the well-being of all creatures (including other human beings). We were created to be God's ambassadors on Earth, to *represent* (not replace) God to all other creatures and to the natural world. We were created "very good" in our essence and purpose.

Now, perhaps, we can begin to see where some of the evil we experience might come from. If *we* fail in our moral obligations, don't we open the door to evil? Clearly, *we* are responsible for at least some of the evil in God's creation—but where did evil originate? How can evil exist if God's creation was made good?

Taking God at His word, everything He created—even Satan—was good at the time of its creation. As a rational being, however, Satan was created with the ability to make intelligent choices and with the freedom to choose to do good … or to do evil. God could have created all beings with no choice other than to obey Him, but that would have made it impossible for them to respond to God in love. Only free, rational beings can choose to love. Out of love, God gave Satan the freedom to choose, even though He already knew that Satan might choose to go his own way in defiance of his Creator's good plan and purpose. When Satan ultimately chose to rebel against God's plan for him and for us, evil entered God's very good creation.[168] So, God didn't create evil; He simply created the freedom that made it possible for evil to exist.

> ### CONSIDER THIS
> God could have created all beings with no choice other than to obey Him, but that would have made it impossible for them to respond to God in love.

Why would God allow such a thing, knowing that Satan's evil choice would ultimately corrupt humanity as well? We are not told directly, but just as it was an act of God's love to create Satan with the freedom to choose to love or to rebel, God created Adam and Eve (and all of us) with that same freedom—the choice to trust and obey God or to believe Satan's lie and reject God's goodness. With the hope that some people would choose to enter into a loving relationship with Him, God created beings with the freedom to reject Him.[169] Similarly, couples choose to have children even though they know their children will often disobey and fail to return their love. Children are generally an expression of a couple's love for one another, a love that parents naturally want to pour out on their offspring, even if it means they will also have many struggles as they raise their children. While they hope their love will be freely returned, parents know there is no guarantee; God knew that as well but, in love, created us anyway, willing to suffer the pain of being rejected.

In summary:

1. Every aspect of the world was "good" when God created, and the whole of creation was "very good." God's personal name is "LORD" (YHWH).

2. Man and woman (Adam and Eve) were created to have a personal relationship with God, given God's spirit, and made to be stewards over God's creation.

3. God provided for every need of the man and the woman, but also established a commandment that they should obey lest they die.

4. The serpent—animated by Satan, an angel—chose to rebel against God's plan for himself and for humanity, tempting Adam and Eve.

5. Evil, the absence of good, infected God's good creation.

6. God knew what would happen, but in order to create beings who were free to respond to Him in love, He allowed for the possibility that Satan (and then Adam and Eve) would choose to reject Him and His purposes for them.

7. Adam and Eve rejected God's good for their *perception* of the good, believing they could have something better.

Humanity Judged (Genesis 3:8-24)

Many people have suffered and still suffer greatly from the evil that God allowed to enter into, and corrupt, His very good creation. Why? Does He have a plan to deal with evil and restore goodness?

What Adam and Eve don't yet understand at this point is that they have dealt a mortal blow to their relationship with God, a blow that will extend to all human beings. They die spiritually, and the innocent fellowship they have with God and with one another is severed. Their choice to distrust God rather than believe that He had provided His best for them becomes a permanent character flaw, a corruption of God's image in them. Complete trust is replaced with doubt of God's love for them, an overriding self-concern blinding them to God's goodness. Fear begins to influence their thoughts and actions, not just how they respond to God but how they relate to one another as well.

Adam and Eve immediately become self-conscious and ashamed of their appearance; they realize for the first time that they are naked and cover themselves with fig leaves.[170] Then, when God calls out to them, they hide themselves.[171] For the first time, they are afraid of God. They are spiritually as well as physically naked, their childlike innocence replaced with shame and guilt. When God asks whether they have eaten of the forbidden fruit,[172] rather than taking responsibility for their disobedience, Adam blames God for giving him Eve and blames Eve for giving him the fruit, and then Eve blames the serpent for lying to her.[173] Adam and Eve try to conceal the truth just as they tried to conceal their nakedness.

As the source of goodness, God cannot allow this evil to exist in His presence, so He pronounces the judgment He had forewarned. Beginning with Satan, the serpent,[174] God declares that he will crawl forevermore on his belly, but the more significant curse is that there will be continual hostility between "[him] and the woman, between [his] offspring and hers." The promised conflict between the offspring of Eve[175] and the offspring of Satan is suggestive of a battle in the spiritual realm. God promises that the offspring of the woman will one day crush the head of the serpent (Satan) but also that he will suffer from the conflict.[176] It seems that God already had in mind a plan to undo the damage to humankind that Satan had caused through Adam and Eve.[177]

Having pronounced judgment on Satan, God next judges the woman, saying first that her pains in childbirth will be greatly increased. Not only is her relationship with God affected, but also her disobedience has consequences in the natural order as well—in this case, making childbearing difficult for herself, and ultimately for all women. Then Eve is told that she will have an excessive desire for her husband, and he will rule over her. That is not the way God intended for the man and woman to relate to one another. He made them in innocence, having no secrets or reason to question the other's love, honesty, or motivations. But with their failure, the trusting relationship between Adam and Eve—as well as that of all future husbands and wives—would become hobbled by self-interest, distrust, and fear. The man had been the leader in their relationship, but the woman was his partner. Just as they had become one flesh in their physical natures,[178] they were to be of one mind and heart, functioning in unity as they fulfilled their respective roles out of love for each other. But their love became distorted when they took what was not rightfully theirs to have. No longer would it be the norm for the woman to trust the man to lead rightly or for the man to work with the woman as his partner. The man begins to exercise unbalanced, authoritative control—rather than healthy leadership—in their relationship, and the woman begins to have an unbalanced, envious desire to take control from—rather than support—her husband.[179]

Last of all, God judges Adam, cursing the ground and turning what was intended to be rewarding, satisfying work into "painful toil." Adam had been the caretaker in the Garden of Eden, freely eating from all but one tree that produced an abundance of fruit, with minimal effort on his part, but now food would be difficult to obtain or find. In a sense, the ground itself rebels against man just as Adam had rebelled against God. Instead of the land naturally producing what the man needs and desires, Adam would now have to fight the land to produce good food, and it would bring forth ugly, useless plants and weeds as well. Worse yet, God declares to Adam, "By the sweat of your brow you will eat your food until you return to the ground, since from it you were taken; for dust you are and to dust you will return."[180] Adam and Eve would suffer physical death as well. Although their spiritual separation was immediate, their physical death would be gradual. Their aging bodies would be an ever-present reminder of their failure, for themselves and for all those who would come after them.

But did the misbehavior of Adam and Eve truly warrant such severe consequences? They ate some fruit that God arbitrarily declared to be off-limits. How bad could that be? Let's step back and look at the big picture: First, God created Adam and Eve to have the privilege of an intimate relationship with Him. Perhaps God even appeared to them in the form of a human being.[181] Whatever the case, it is clear that God desired to have a personal, caring relationship with Adam and Eve. Consistent with His care, God placed them in a pristine setting where they had satisfying work, desirable food, and sexual pleasure—everything they truly needed and much more. It was only the *one* tree in the Garden that was off-limits out of a *multitude* of trees to choose from.

Satan was right when he told Eve that she would become "like God knowing good and evil," but he failed to explain to Eve that there was a good reason God had created human beings *apart from* the knowledge of evil. As time- and space-limited beings, we were not created with the capacity to handle evil's deceitful destructiveness, such as the desire to make gods of ourselves, to direct our own lives apart from the goodness of the God who created us, and to believe that we know what is best for ourselves. Tragically, tempted by the promise of "more," Adam and Eve fell for the lie that they were being cheated by the very One who had freely given them so much. Despite all evidence to the contrary, they chose to believe—and their actions declared—that the God who had created and loved them was a liar, purposely keeping His best from them. While it is true that the serpent planted the seeds of distrust in their hearts—for which God promised that Satan would one day pay dearly—the serpent did not *force* them to choose wrongly. They always remained responsible for their actions, for their obedience (or lack of) to God's command. Forsaking God's good in order to know good *and* evil, they received what they desired: the opportunity to experience evil in body (pain in giving birth), mind (toil), and spirit (separation from God). Their children would be born with that same damaged relationship with God and with one another as well. It seemed that Satan had indeed permanently dethroned humankind from their rightful place in God's order.

God had not prohibited Adam and Eve from gaining knowledge, but God was to be the One who would answer all of their questions. Everything they would have learned from God would have been beneficial for them in body, mind and spirit, and favorable for their surroundings (the land, plants, and creatures). Just as young children trust their parents to protect and provide for them, and good parents make it possible for their children to trust them and to grow in knowledge and maturity, Adam and Eve were to have that kind of relationship with God. As they received good things from God, they would have been filled with thanksgiving for all of His blessings and would have been a blessing to others and to creation. But when they chose to wrest control of their lives from God, they made "gods" of themselves, becoming their own protectors, providers, and masters of their future … but without the knowledge, wisdom, foresight, or power to fill those God-sized shoes. The temptation to distrust God, to satisfy our personal desires when and as *we* please, has become a problem for all humanity.

Evil had infected the world in general and human nature in particular; Adam and Eve were to blame, but every child since then has been born a natural participant in their failure. How bad were the effects? We read in Genesis 6:5 that after many generations, "The LORD saw how great the wickedness of the human race had become on the earth, and that every inclination of the thoughts of the human heart was only evil all the time." Because Adam and Eve died spiritually, cast out from the place of intimate fellowship with God, each of us—their offspring—is born physically alive but spiritually dead,[182] alienated from God and cut off from the hope of eternal life that was supposed to have been the destiny of all humanity. Worse still, apart from God's protection and an intimate, loving relationship with Him, we instead develop an intimate connection with and uncontrollable taste for evil. Having inherited Adam's selfish desire to control our own lives, to be our own gods, we are born physically, emotionally, psychologically, and spiritually naked before God.

It was a slow process, probably taking hundreds of years, but God's heart was broken,[183] and He could no longer withhold judgment, a judgment that is hard for us to comprehend in its scope and severity—the destruction of all but one family of the human race by a flood (Gen. 6:7-8, 17).[184] The Noahic flood is just one of several severe judgments by God in the Old Testament, judgments that are abhorrent to our modern sensitivities, so much so that many people outright reject the God of the Bible as a monster. Clearly, God's judgments aren't agreeable; but it would seem that He wants us to see them as the horror that they are and as warnings that we are on the wrong path. This is a difficult and complex topic, one for which no explanation is likely to fully satisfy us, but lest we miss the irony, let us remember that at the core of the evil of Eden is the distrust of God. We appointed ourselves as judges of what is good and right, so it isn't surprising that we also accuse God of injustice when He judges evil. Our complaints about God's judgments are sometimes more about our refusal to trust and submit to God, to blame God rather than accept responsibility for what we and others have done.

We simply cannot know all that God knows about the extent of evil and what should be done about it. While God is fully aware of the consequences for *all* humanity and the physical world as a result of *every* evil act committed over the course of *all* human history, we cannot fully comprehend the effects of even a single evil act. For example, it is widely understood that victims of violent crimes can also be seriously harmed emotionally and

> At the core of the evil of Eden is the distrust of God.

psychologically. Family members and close friends are also impacted by the suffering inflicted upon their loved ones. Even people who read or hear about the incident may be negatively affected, feeling a heightened sense of fear and anger. Victims of crime often have difficulty connecting with people as they try to cope and heal. Residual consequences might also propagate to later generations, especially if the victims have children. A single act of evil can ultimately cause ripple effects in generations that have no awareness of the original evil act. If we cannot understand the extent of evil in the world, how can we justly accuse God of injustice when He judges? It makes no sense to blame God for the evil that affects us all—and for which we are at least partially responsible—and then condemn Him when we are repulsed by His judgment of that evil.

CONSIDER THIS

If we cannot understand the extent of evil in the world, how can we justly accuse God of injustice when He judges?

It makes no sense to blame God for the evil that affects us all—and for which we are at least partially responsible—and then condemn Him when we are repulsed by His judgment of that evil.

Thankfully, as awful as were the consequences of Adam and Eve's disobedience, God's purpose for humanity—to be in relationship with Him—was not permanently thwarted by Satan or by the subsequent evil of the human race that Satan's deception brought about. Instead, God promised that He would one day destroy evil and secure humanity's redemption.

In summary:

1. Adam and Eve disobey God and experience immediate spiritual death as a result, a corruption of their intimate, trusting relationship with God and with one another. As a result of their disobedience, we too are all born into spiritual death, separated from God and having little to no concern for His ways.

2. Their loss of innocence manifests itself in guilt (hiding from God), failure to take responsibility for their own actions (lying), and selfishness replacing selfless love as the motivation for their actions.

3. God pronounces judgment on the serpent (Satan) first, then Eve, and then Adam.

4. Adam and Eve experience God's judgment through suffering in various ways during their lives and ultimately by physical death, as God had promised.

5. While it may seem at first that God overreacted to the disobedience of Adam and Eve, a thorough analysis reveals the astonishing extent of the evil that resulted, and the righteousness of God's judgment.

6. In judging the serpent, God promises that an offspring of Eve would one day crush the serpent at the cost of his own suffering, the suggestion being that the evil caused by the serpent (Satan) would be turned back on the serpent, reversing the fortunes of humanity.

God's image and likeness in us has not been eradicated, but we are no longer born into an unhindered relationship with Him. We have continued in Adam and Eve's legacy; having the *illusion* of control over our lives, we consistently reject God's ways for our own. We like to think of ourselves as the "captain of our own ship," but that prideful attitude loses its luster when tragedy strikes or someone harms us and we can do nothing to stop our suffering. We all want God to address the evil in others but not in us, but it doesn't work that way. Adam and Eve may have been to blame for inviting evil into our world, but *we* have followed in their footsteps. Our communication lines with God were damaged by the actions of Adam and Eve so that we have neither the ability nor, it seems, the desire to make repairs of our own initiative. Consequently, with every evil thought, word, and deed, we grow further removed from God as individuals, as a society, and as a human race. Nevertheless, even though we bring this evil on ourselves, God has promised to redeem us, to reestablish the relationship we were always meant to have with Him, as the same one Adam and Eve experienced prior to their rebellion.

Has He done so?

We now turn our attention to the rest of the Bible to find the answer to this question and what it might mean for us.

9
The Redeemer Lives

> "There is no prophesy
> like the promises of God."
> Lailah Gifty Akita

In Chapter 8, we saw that God had promised to redeem humankind, to reestablish the relationship we were always meant to have with Him. But has He done so? In this chapter, we will see how God prepared the long-waiting people of Israel for their Redeemer, and then brought Him forth in the person of Jesus.

The Back Story

Genesis 3:15 prophesied the coming of Someone who would "crush the serpent's head," defeating our spiritual enemy (Satan) and making possible the restoration of fellowship with God.[185] The specifics of God's plan for the redemption of humanity wouldn't be completely known for thousands of years, but that plan is gradually revealed through the Hebrew Scriptures.

God begins to differentiate between peoples when He established His covenant with Noah, telling him to build an ark to save his family and all wildlife. It would be through Noah's descendants that the promised Redeemer would come. Subsequently, God called Abram (later named Abraham) and promised—long before Abram had any offspring to receive and carry forth God's promise—that all families of the earth would be blessed through him;[186] twenty-five years later, Isaac was born to then-elderly Abraham and Sarah as the beginning of the fulfillment of God's promise. It was through Isaac and his offspring that God would bless the world.[187]

God's promise continued through Jacob, Isaac's son, who was renamed "Israel" and through whom came the twelve tribes of Israel, the Israelites. The Israelites were God's anointed, the recipients of the promise, and the means of God's blessing to the world. When Israel blessed his sons, he prophesied that the ruler of God's people would come from the tribe of Judah.[188]

Promise of a Ruler to Come

Hundreds of years later, God called Moses to lead His people, to be the instrument by which God would save His people from Egypt and bring them to a land of promise. After being delivered from Egypt, God gave Moses the Ten Commandments and the sacrificial system, to teach God's people how they were to behave toward one another and in worship of God. Before he died, Moses told the Israelites that God would raise up another leader like him, a prophet to whom they would listen, who would tell them what God wanted them to know, just as Moses did.[189]

Jumping another several hundred years forward, the Israelites began asking for a king so that they could be like all the other nations around them. God warned them about what they could expect of an earthly king, but He gave them what they wanted. Every king thereafter was viewed as anointed by God, and the people began to expect that the ruler to come would be a king of some kind, perhaps because King David was promised an heir whose kingdom would last forever. Years later, King Ahaz was told that a virgin would conceive and give birth to a son who would be called "Immanuel," which means "God with us." At other times in Israel (during the reigns of Kings Jotham, Ahaz, and Hezekiah), the prophet Micah said that a ruler would come whose origin was prophesied long ago. He would lead (shepherd) His people "in the strength of the LORD, in the majesty of the name of the LORD His God" and "shall be great to the ends of the earth." Not only that, but "He [*himself*] shall be their peace."[190] While that person is not named, it is clear that the promised ruler to come was to be Someone with unusual, possibly even Divine, characteristics and scope of impact.[191]

Prophets continued to speak to Israel of the ruler to come, filling out the picture of the kind of leader that Israel should expect:[192]

- Isaiah prophesied the coming of a servant who would be filled with the Spirit of God, through whom God would establish true justice on Earth.

- God's servant would be righteous before God and yet suffer, being rejected by His own people.

- He would be crushed according to God's will, for the guilt of humanity.

- Yet, His death would not be the end because "He shall see His offspring." God "shall prolong His days," and "the will of the Lord shall prosper in His hand."

- Not only that, but His suffering would somehow "make many to be accounted righteous," and God would therefore "divide Him a portion with the many," sharing the spoils of His victory with His allies—those to be accounted righteous.

- He would be anointed with the Spirit of God for the purpose of bringing good news to the poor and liberty to the captives, declaring the year of the Lord's favor.

Continued Reminders of the Promise

Despite the continual plea of the prophets, rebellious Israel failed to return to its God, and the people suffered destruction and exile at the hands of their enemies, the Assyrians and Babylonians. But God did not forget them or His promise:[193]

- Jeremiah prophesied that God would make a new covenant with the people of Israel and with the people of Judah; He would "forgive their iniquity, and ... will remember their sin no more."

- God's prophets continued to point to and paint a picture of the One who would "bruise [the serpent's] head." He would be "one like a son of man," but He would come "with the clouds of heaven" and be presented to God ("the Ancient of Days"), where He would be given an everlasting dominion over all peoples, nations, and languages.

- Later in Daniel, we read of an "anointed one" (Hebrew: "Messiah"; Greek: "Christ") who would bring in everlasting righteousness. While there are various interpretations of this prophecy, one possibility is that the anointed one who was to be cut off would be the crucified Messiah.

- Further, the king to come would bring salvation with Him, a king who would bring peace to the nations and who would rule "from sea to sea, and from the River to the ends of the earth."

All these prophetic words pointed to a ruler who would bring peace, salvation, and restoration to the Israelites *and a way for all other people groups* to have a proper relationship with God.

But has the promised Redeemer come, or are we still waiting for Him?

The Redeemer Revealed

The Bible's New Testament opens with four books called the Gospels documenting the life of a man named Jesus who lived in Israel approximately 2,000 years ago.[194] Each Gospel describes the life of Jesus from the perspective of its author, and how Jesus fulfilled the promises of the Hebrew Scriptures as the long-awaited Redeemer of Israel and, to the surprise of many first-century Jewish people, *all humanity*—people from every nation, even those who had been enemies of Israel and its God. A separate New Testament book, Acts of the Apostles, picks up the story after Jesus's earthly life, recounting how the news about Jesus spread from first century Israel to the entire Roman Empire. Of the remaining New Testament writings, most are letters from apostles and other early leaders to New Testament churches addressing the difficulties and concerns of the growing number of people who had come to believe in Jesus as their Redeemer—both Jews and Gentiles alike.[195] The final book,

Revelation, primarily portrays world-ending future events associated with Jesus's role as Judge and Redeemer.

The Gospels of Matthew, Mark, Luke, and John were not written during Jesus's lifetime. People were not appointed from Jesus's birth to record the significant events of His life. Like every biography, Jesus's life only became worthy of investigation and description because of what He said and did, and the impact He had on the world He lived in and beyond (both geographically and temporally). The Gospels and the Jesus they proclaim do not stand alone, disconnected from the history of the people of Israel. Rather, the Gospels declare the fulfillment of all that was promised before, not only to Israel but also to all humankind. Although it was only in retrospect that the prophetic words of the Hebrew Scriptures were attributed to Jesus, the Gospel writers looked back on Jesus's life and recognized that it embodied *and* accomplished all that was promised by those prophecies.

Whatever we might believe about Jesus, those who wrote about Him did not offer the option of regarding Him merely as a good teacher or worldly wise philosopher.[196] The Gospels recorded assertions by Jesus of a unique Son-to-Father relationship with God, claims that the Gospel authors supported with accounts of miraculous healings and displays of power and authority that, if true, could only be attributed to a person somehow directed or empowered by Divinity, or to Divinity itself.[197]

> The Gospels declare the fulfillment of all that was promised before, not only to Israel but also to all humankind.

Still, if Jesus's death had merely been the conclusion to His life, it's likely that no one would have written about Him, except perhaps as a warning against trusting charismatic leaders who make bizarre claims about themselves. But His death was not the final word. Along with their extraordinary accounts of Jesus's life and teachings, His followers claimed that He came back to life on the third day following His death and that He empowered and commissioned them to proclaim Him as Redeemer. It would be easy to dismiss these stories as the fantastical tales of uneducated first century fishermen except that they have survived every attempt to discredit them for the past 2,000 years.

Who is this Jesus? Why would anyone even begin to think that He might be the Redeemer? To answer these questions, we need to start by considering what Jesus's biographers (the Gospel authors) have written about Him.

CONSIDER THIS

It would be easy to dismiss the Gospels as the fantastical tales of uneducated first century fishermen except that they have survived every attempt to discredit them for the past 2,000 years.

10
The Witness of the Gospels

The Gospel stories ask us to believe extraordinary things about Jesus: the miracles He performed, the words He spoke about Himself, and—most significant for us—His role in the redemption of human beings. What follows is a summary of the Gospel witness; however, a categorized listing of Bible verses that each point to an aspect of Jesus's nature, actions, or teaching may be found in Appendix D: The Gospels' Description of Jesus. Once we have established what the Gospels say about Jesus, we will look at the post-resurrection claims of His disciples and then consider what that means for us.

Jesus's Human Nature

Regarding Jesus's humanity, the Gospels depict a man with normal human emotions, who relates to others much as we would. One event described in John 11:1-44 provides an intimate glimpse into Jesus's human nature: Lazarus, the brother of Martha and Mary, was ill, so his sisters sent for Jesus to come and heal him. But Jesus delayed, having Divine insight that God intended to perform a greater miracle than merely delivering Lazarus from his illness. Lazarus had died by the time Jesus arrived on scene, but Lazarus's sisters desperately hung onto belief that Jesus could still do something for their brother. Seeing the sisters and those who had come to pay their respects weeping, and seeing the tomb where

Lazarus had been laid, Jesus was deeply moved in spirit and wept. And then, deeply moved with compassion, Jesus prayed for Lazarus's resurrection and called him out of the tomb. Notwithstanding His prophetic pronouncements or the miraculous raising of Lazarus, we are given no reason to think that Jesus's humanity is swallowed up by what appears to be His access to Divine power; rather, His Divine attributes seem to function naturally within the limits of His human body and intellect. That is, as described by the Gospel writers, Jesus is a normal man of godly character but—unlike the rest of us—He has constant, unfettered access to the insight, wisdom, and power of God, and He is without sin.[198]

It is not surprising that the Gospels do not dwell on Jesus's *human* nature. The Gospel writers do not need to prove something that the reader would assume to be true. On the other hand, Matthew 1:1-17 importantly connects Jesus's human origins to Abraham and David in fulfillment of the promises made to them. Luke 3:23-38 takes a different approach, tracing Jesus's human origins back to Adam, the first man, but goes further to suggest that Jesus has a Divine pedigree.

It is actually Jesus's *Divine* nature that is unexpected and questioned and to which the Gospel writers devote most of their testimony. Nonetheless, it is important to understand that Jesus was fully human; otherwise, it is hard to see how He could be the One promised in Genesis 3:15, Someone born of a woman who could be hurt ("bruised") by Satan. Further, if God could have simply forgiven and restored humankind to its privileged position by Divine edict, then there would not have been any reason for a redeemer or savior to be born. That suggests that Jesus's humanity may play a more important role in God's plan to redeem humankind than we might think at first, which will become more clear as we continue to examine the witness of the Gospels and the post-resurrection understanding of the early believers.

Jesus's Divine Nature

Jesus's Divinely suggestive words and actions, and especially His alleged Divine nature, are the portions of the Gospels (as well as the other New Testament writings) that many people find difficult to believe and are rightly subject to the greatest scrutiny. None of us were eyewitnesses to these events. Nor do we have a recording or video of "Today's Gospel News" like we might today; instead, the primary witness to Jesus's life is provided by Jesus's disciples and those who followed afterward.

The following overview highlights some of the important aspects of Jesus's life and teachings.

The Life and Teachings of Jesus

Jesus Supernaturally Conceived

Born of a woman, the Gospels testify that Jesus entered the world as fully human but exists eternally as the Divine Son of God through whom all things were made. While it's difficult enough to believe that Jesus might have a Divine nature, the idea that He came into this world with a dual nature (Divine *and* human) is beyond human comprehension.[199] But Jesus's Divine nature is crucial to His being able to fulfill the Redeemer role; otherwise, He Himself would have needed a redeemer. While the Old Testament details remained obscure, the Messiah's birth, Divine lineage, and destiny should not have come as a complete surprise to the people of Israel, having been prophesied in various ways throughout the Hebrew Scriptures (Dan. 9:25-26). Still, it seems that the people were not ready for Jesus's earthly appearance and claims to Messiahship, in part because it had been some 400 years since the last prophetic promise of His coming, but likely also because there was no clear understanding of what to expect of a Messiah. The prophecies about Jesus became clear only after He fulfilled them.[200]

According to Scripture, the conception of Jesus by the Holy Spirit in the Virgin Mary's womb was prophetically announced to

Mary by the angel Gabriel and later to Joseph. The angel also told Mary that Jesus would be called "holy —the Son of God," suggesting a personal, familial relationship with God (Isa. 7:14, Matt. 1:18-23). His words and actions would one day be a witness to His Divine origin, and Jesus would be given "the throne of His father David and … reign over the house of Jacob forever, and of His kingdom there [would] be no end."[201] After Jesus's birth in Bethlehem (Mic. 5:2, Matt. 2:6), when Mary and Joseph presented Him in the Temple, a devout man named Simeon encountered the parents and referred to Jesus as God's salvation, not only for Israel but for the Gentiles as well (that is, for all people), and he warned Mary and Joseph that Jesus would be opposed by many in Israel. Then a prophetess named Anna suggested by her giving thanks to God that Jesus was integral to God's plan for redemption of Jerusalem—a metaphorical way of referring to Israel; later we find twelve-year-old Jesus amazing the religious teachers with His spiritual understanding and even referring to the Temple as "My Father's house," indicating an understanding of His familial connection to God himself.[202]

Jesus Anointed for Ministry

Jesus's public ministry began at the age of 30 following His baptism by John the Baptist, after which "a voice from heaven declares, 'This is my beloved Son, with whom I am well pleased.'" Jesus subsequently spent 40 days in the Judean wilderness fasting and praying, where He was tempted by the devil but did not succumb as Adam and Eve did. He then returned to Galilee in the power of the Spirit and began His teaching ministry where He claimed that the promise of Isaiah 61:1-2 was fulfilled in Him. At this point, Jesus began to recruit twelve disciples; others would follow, but the twelve were specifically called as His closest confidants. Shortly thereafter, at the wedding feast in Cana, Jesus performed the first of His signs, turning water into wine, at which point His disciples believed in Him, presumably as the expected Messiah.[203]

As John the Baptist continued his own work, he prepared the way for Jesus's ministry, proclaiming a baptism of repentance for the forgiveness of sins, teaching that the true descendants of Abraham—those who would receive and carry on the promises given to Abraham—were those who confessed their sins and did what was right in their relationships with others. Jesus expanded the scope of John's teaching to speak in terms of the good news of a coming kingdom, which was Jesus's proclamation that the kingdom of God (the reign of God on Earth) was open to those who choose to enter, who desire a restored relationship with God through repentance and belief.[204] But belief in what? Belief that "Jesus is the Christ, the Son of God, and that by believing [the hearer] may have life in His name." Jesus would ultimately give His life on the cross to pay the penalty for humanity's rebellion against God, and He would be raised from the dead as confirmation that His words were true and His sacrifice was acceptable. In the meantime, Jesus reinforced His message by healing diseases and afflictions among the people. He told John's disciples to "go and tell John what you have seen and heard: the blind receive their sight, the lame walk, lepers are cleansed, and the deaf hear, the dead are raised up, the poor have good news preached to them."[205]

Jesus Proclaims the Coming Kingdom

As Jesus and His disciples traveled around preaching, large crowds of people followed, attracted by His teaching and the authority with which He spoke, and by the accompanying miraculous healings. Jesus announced that there was a coming kingdom in which God reigned on Earth and in heaven. The authority with which He spoke about Himself and the Father's purposes for Him suggested a much more intimate relationship with God the Father than the people were accustomed to. Soon, the people began to wonder whether Jesus could be the Messiah; even many of the authorities believed in Him, but they were afraid of the powerful Pharisees, so they refrained from saying anything, not wanting to be kicked out of the synagogue. The religious leaders were not without reason to be uncertain, even skeptical, of Jesus, and it would not be until after His death that they began to fully grasp how Jesus fulfilled the Messianic prophecies. In fact, the foremost religious leaders would ultimately refuse to believe what Jesus's teachings and miracles revealed about Him; their hearts were so hardened against the truth that they even became furious with Jesus for healing people on the Sabbath. They did not dispute the reality of the miracles, but they could not accept that Jesus had come from God and was doing exactly what God the Father had wanted Him to do.[206]

Not only did the miracles point to the relationship that Jesus had with God as His Father, but His teaching and proclamation of the kingdom of God did as well. Jesus's moral teaching challenged the people, especially the religious leaders, to hear and obey the moral law—the Ten Commandments—with their heart. Jesus was more interested in their relationships with one another and with God than with their fulfilling a checklist of legal "dos and don'ts." Five times He told the people, "You have heard it said ... but I say to you," teaching with an authority reserved only for God. In the famous Sermon on the Mount, Jesus called the people to a deeper, more personal understanding and practice of God's Law, one that aligned with the true purpose of the Commandments, which was to provide a right framework for a proper relationship with God and one another. The people were rightly curious about what this meant for salvation, having been taught a particular way by the religious leaders; when someone asked whether the saved would be few, Jesus replied, "Strive to enter through the narrow door. For many, I tell you, will seek to enter and will not be able."

Who or what is the narrow door? Jesus told Thomas, "I am the way, and the truth, and the life. No one comes to the Father except through me." Jesus is the narrow door, the Redeemer of humankind.[207]

Jesus Challenges the Religious Authorities

But a storm was brewing, and the religious leaders were becoming increasingly angry at Jesus's challenges to their authority, as well as His condemnation of their rules and practices that ignored the needs of the people and circumvented God's purposes. Rather than respond in repentance, they became more indignant and sought ways to trap Him in His words, and even to kill Him. Jesus was well aware that the religious leaders were plotting against Him. Moreover, He told the disciples at least three times during the course of His ministry that He would be betrayed into the hands of men, and that He would suffer and be crucified but would be raised up on the third day. While this confused the disciples at the time, Jesus said He was doing the will of God and that His death would be in accordance with His Father's—that is, God's—plan. Knowing that the people did not truly grasp who He was and God's purpose for Him, Jesus emphatically declared Himself to be one with the Father as the Father's Divine Son. He was clear that He is the Messiah, the Savior of the world. Not surprisingly, Jesus's claims led to charges of blasphemy. It was clear, though, that the religious leaders were actually more concerned about their positions than about God's honor, and that they wanted Jesus eliminated to avoid antagonizing their Roman masters.[208]

Knowing what was about to happen to Him, Jesus celebrated the Passover meal with His disciples. It was during that meal that Jesus told His disciples, "One of you will betray me." As the disciples wondered which of them would do such a thing, Jesus pointed to Judas. Judas denied it, but Satan entered him, and he left to lead the religious authorities to Jesus (Ps. 41:9, Zech. 11:12, Matt. 26:14-16, John 13:18). After the Passover supper, Jesus and His disciples went to the Garden of Gethsemane on the Mount of Olives. Knowing that He would soon be arrested, beaten, and crucified, Jesus prayed in great distress to God, His Father, that He might be spared this suffering. Despite the great temptation to save Himself—knowing He could call on legions of angels for His deliverance—Jesus chose to submit to the Father's plan out of love for us, saying, "not as I will, but as You will."[209]

Jesus Arrested

Judas led the soldiers to Jesus, who was arrested and taken to the courtyard of the high priest, but the disciples fled as Jesus predicted, afraid of being arrested along with Him. Being known to the high priest, however, John was able to safely follow; Peter entered the courtyard with John but denied even knowing Jesus the three times he was asked.[210] He departed in shame, realizing he had failed Jesus, just as Jesus had warned.[211]

As the trial proceeded, the religious leaders showed that they were fully aware of the people's beliefs about Jesus, demanding that He swear whether He was the Christ, the Son of God.[212] They were jealous of Jesus's following and angry that the people's beliefs about Him challenged their authority. In addition, they were looking for justification to condemn Him out of fear that their current stable relationship with their Roman masters would be disrupted if Jesus was not stopped and a riot ensued. The religious leaders fully expected Jesus to acknowledge the claims He made about Himself, but they were shocked when He suggested that *they* knew the claims were true ("You have said so") and then added, "from now on you will see the Son of Man seated at the right hand of power and coming on the clouds of heaven"—a clear claim to Divinity. Having heard what they believed to be outright blasphemy, the leaders condemned Jesus to death in their own council and then brought Him to Pilate, the Roman governor, to carry out the sentence they desired.[213]

While Pilate rightly judged that Jesus was innocent of violating Roman laws and that the religious leaders were acting out of their own jealousy, the leaders stirred up the crowds and demanded Jesus's crucifixion saying, "We have a law, and according to that law He ought to die because He has made himself the Son of God." Pilate ultimately complied when it became clear that he could not dissuade the crowd; he was afraid that the people would accuse him of disloyalty to the emperor and start a riot (Isa. 53:3, Mark 15:13-32). By Pilate's order, Jesus was whipped and led away to be crucified (Ps. 22, Isa. 53:4-5, Zech. 13:7, Matt. 26:31, Matt. 27:26).[214]

Jesus Crucified

Jesus was crucified along with two criminals. Some of the onlookers mocked Him, calling on Him to save Himself if He was the person He claimed to be, thus showing that they were well aware of Jesus's claims and felt vindicated. Jesus's mother and the other women who had been with and supported Him watched from a distance—John was there, but the other disciples were too afraid to be associated with Jesus. From the cross, Jesus verbally forgave His executioners and those who condemned Him, saying that they acted in ignorance. Darkness came over the land for three hours, and when He died, Jesus intentionally—in full control of this life—gave up His spirit to His Father: The earth shook, and the curtain of the Temple was torn in two from top to bottom.[215] Although crucifixion was common, Jesus's manner of death was so unlike others that a centurion witness declared, "Certainly this man was innocent!" and "Truly this man was the Son of God!"[216]

Since that was the Day of Preparation for the Passover, the religious leaders asked Pilate to break the legs of the crucified men so that they would die and could be removed before the Sabbath began. So a soldier broke the legs of both criminals—ensuring a quick if torturous death by suffocation since they could no longer push themselves up by their feet to breathe—but seeing that Jesus was already dead, the soldier did not break Jesus's legs but thrust his spear into Jesus's side; blood and water flowed out according to John, a clear indication that Jesus had died (Ps. 22:16, Zech. 12:10, John 19:34-37).[217] Joseph of Arimathea asked Pilate for Jesus's body. While Pilate was surprised that Jesus was already dead, he ordered that the body be given to Joseph after receiving confirmation from the centurion. Joseph and Nicodemus wrapped the body with linen cloths and spices and placed it in Joseph's own tomb; a large, heavy boulder was rolled into place to cover the entrance and to keep animals out (Isa. 53:9, Matt. 27:57-60). The women (also disciples of Jesus) watched as He was placed in Joseph's tomb, knowing they would have to return once the Sabbath was over to properly finish the burial preparations.[218]

The leaders were well aware of Jesus's claim that He would rise from the dead in three days, so they requested a guard from Pilate to ensure that Jesus's disciples could not steal the body and then claim that He was risen. So, Pilate authorized the leaders to take a guard and seal the stone.[219]

Jesus Resurrected

On the third day (the first day of the week, Sunday), the women returned to the tomb to complete Jesus's burial preparation.[220] Although the Gospel accounts differ somewhat as to the details of what happened and the order of their occurrence, the following are the highlights in approximate sequence:[221]

1. The boulder had been moved from the tomb entrance. Matthew attributes it to a violent earthquake and an angel moving it, but the other Gospels merely say there was already access to the tomb when the women arrived. The guards were so frightened that they became like dead men, unable to move. Matthew's Gospel explained that the guards were bribed by the religious authorities to spread a story that Jesus's body was stolen by the disciples.

2. The women found the stone rolled away.

3. Jesus was not in the tomb.

4. The women were reminded of what Jesus had told them, that He would rise from the dead on the third day.

5. The women went to tell the disciples what they had seen and heard.

6. Jesus revealed Himself to the women in His resurrected body.

7. The women worshipped Jesus.

8. Jesus told the women not to be afraid, but to go and tell the disciples that they would soon see Him.

9. Peter and John ran to the tomb to see if what they had been told was true.

On that same day, Jesus met up with two disciples on the road to Emmaus, where He began to explain how the Scriptures are fulfilled in Him.[222] When Jesus agreed to stay with them that evening, He revealed Himself in the blessing and breaking of the bread; the disciples' eyes were opened to recognize Him, and He disappeared at that moment. When the two disciples returned to Jerusalem and found the others (Judas having committed suicide) hidden for fear of the Jewish religious leaders, they were told that the Lord had appeared to Simon (Peter). The two disciples told their story of knowing the resurrected Jesus in the breaking of the bread, and just then, Jesus appeared to them again.[223] Knowing they were disturbed at His appearing, wanting to believe but unable to grasp what they were seeing, Jesus calmed their fears and concerns by demonstrating that He was truly flesh and bones—not a disembodied spirit— showing them the wounds in His hands and feet, and eating the fish they provided.[224]

Jesus the Redeemer

Over the course of the next 40 days, Jesus taught His disciples "that everything written about Him in the Law of Moses and the Prophets and the Psalms had to be fulfilled," and that the Messiah had to suffer, die, and rise again on the third day. As witnesses to Jesus's life, death, and resurrection, Jesus told them that they were to proclaim to all nations repentance in His name for the forgiveness of sins, so that people everywhere might believe in Him as the Christ, the Son of God, and that by believing they might have eternal life in His name. But they were not to go out until they were clothed with power from on high, that is, with the Holy Spirit.[225]

The Gift of the Holy Spirit

The Gospels document the life, death, and resurrection of Jesus, and some of Jesus's final commands to His disciples before His ascension (His return, that is) to His Father. The book of Acts picks up the story at this point and provides a broad-brush picture of the spread of the Gospel after the disciples are filled with the Holy Spirit.[226]

Even after those 40 days following Jesus's resurrection, some of the disciples still doubted that He was the Messiah, the Son of God, but those who believed worshipped Him.[227] Nevertheless, Jesus reaffirmed His commissioning of the disciples, telling them, "[Make] disciples of all nations, baptizing them in the name of the Father and of the Son and of the Holy Spirit, [and] teaching them to observe all that I have commanded you." Having said these things, Jesus blessed the disciples and ascended to His Father.[228]

As the disciples waited for the Holy Spirit to come, they devoted themselves to prayer and chose Matthias to replace Judas. On the Day of Pentecost, ten days after Jesus's ascension, while the disciples were together in one place, the Holy Spirit was poured out on them, accompanied by spectacular manifestations—the disciples prophesying and praising God in the languages of the foreign visitors to Jerusalem—clearly meant to signify the presence of the power of God. When those present in Jerusalem for the Feast of Pentecost were attracted to the commotion, Peter explained to them that what they were witnessing was what God promised to His people, that "in the last days it shall be ... that I will pour out my Spirit on all flesh" and "everyone who calls upon the name of the Lord shall be saved."[229]

Peter goes on to tell them:

> Jesus of Nazareth, a man attested to you by God with mighty works and wonders and signs that God did through Him in your midst, as you yourselves know—this Jesus, delivered up according to the definite plan and foreknowledge of God, you crucified and

killed by the hands of lawless men. God raised Him up, loosing the pangs of death, because it was not possible for Him to be held by it.[230]

Therefore, "Let all the house of Israel … know for certain that God has made Him both Lord and Christ, this Jesus whom you crucified." Many of the people were cut to the heart, and 3,000 people confessed belief in Jesus and were baptized.[231]

The new believers met together, dedicating themselves to "the apostles teaching and the fellowship, to the breaking of bread and the prayers. And awe came upon every soul, and many wonders and signs were being done through the apostles." Initially referred to as "the Way" and considered a sect within Judaism, the believers continued to grow in number.[232]

As the apostles Peter and John proclaimed Jesus as Lord and Savior, a man more than 40 years of age who had been lame from birth was healed, providing an opportunity for Peter to preach the Gospel to those who witnessed the healing, bringing many more to the faith. The religious leaders arrested the apostles, however, angered that they were proclaiming in Jesus the resurrection from the dead. When they were brought before the council of religious leaders, the apostles boldly proclaimed Jesus as the way of salvation, and when they were told not to speak or teach at all in the name of Jesus, they responded: "Whether it is right in the sight of God to listen to you rather than to God, you must judge, for we cannot but speak of what we have seen and heard." Because the leaders could not deny that a significant sign had been performed, they threatened the apostles and let them go.[233]

Despite attempts by the religious leaders to quash the spread of the Gospel, the number of believers continued to grow until a Pharisee named Saul approved of the murder of the deacon Stephen and sought to arrest those who professed belief in Jesus. But Saul had a vision of the resurrected Jesus and came to faith in Christ, no longer able to deny the truth of the Gospel. He was called by Jesus to proclaim the Gospel to the Gentiles and took on a new name, "Paul." As documented throughout the book of Acts, Paul ultimately spread the Gospel to much of the Roman Empire during his three missionary journeys, and great numbers of people came to faith in Christ.[234]

The apostle Peter brought many Jewish people to the faith just as the apostle Paul brought many Gentiles to find eternal life in Jesus. The other apostles and disciples did the same, but the book of Acts focused on the actions of these two most prominent apostles. They preached Jesus as the Redeemer of humankind, defeating sin and death, promising the Holy Spirit to those who place their faith in Jesus as their Lord and Savior.[235]

Christianity has faced challenges from within and without throughout its entire 2,000-year history, but the number of professing Christians has continued to grow to its currently estimated 2.2 billion (32 percent of the world population).[236]

But why should we believe that the claims of the Bible are true?

To that question we now turn.

11
Reasons to Believe

> "The center of salvation is the Cross of
> Jesus, and the reason it is so easy
> to obtain salvation is
> because it cost God so much."
> Oswald Chambers

Is Jesus the Redeemer?

Is Jesus the promised Redeemer of humankind in fulfillment of the promises of the Hebrew Scriptures? The Gospels and the other writings of the New Testament certainly make that claim, but why should we believe that these claims are true?

While there are different lines of inquiry that someone could take in addressing this question, we will focus on the singular critical event—Jesus's resurrection. Our acceptance of the Resurrection depends in part on whether we accept the Gospel accounts as truthful, but our belief in the truth of the Gospels depends in large measure on whether we believe that Jesus *actually* rose from the dead. As the Apostle Paul says, "And if Christ has not been raised, your faith is futile and you are still in your sins."[237] But if Jesus did rise from the dead, then His resurrection validates His teachings and His claims to a relationship with God and ought to be taken seriously.[238]

Is the Resurrection True?

Did Jesus rise from the dead? While it cannot be proven as an indisputable fact, just as much of what we take to be true is founded on some element of belief, the circumstantial evidence seems to support the truth of Jesus's resurrection.

We have already established that it is more likely than not that God created the world and all life. If that is true, then the Resurrection of Jesus would be well within the realm of God's powers, even if it is hard for us to imagine. The God who created life in the first place would surely be able to renew life in a dead person.

Prophecies Fulfilled

As we discussed in the previous chapter, the major events of Jesus's life, including His death and resurrection, were prophesied about Him as the Messiah of the Hebrew Scriptures. The eight most definitive of the Messianic prophecies include:

- Birth in Bethlehem (Mic. 5:2, Matt. 2:6)
- Events leading to Jesus's birth (Dan. 9:25, Gen. 49:10)
- Virgin birth and Divine attribution (Isa. 7:14, Matt. 1:18-23)
- Betrayal (Ps. 41:9, Zech. 11:12, Matt. 26:14-16, John 13:18)
- Manner of death (Ps. 22, Isa. 53:4-5, Zech. 13:7, Matt. 26:31, Matt. 27:26)
- Rejection by His own people and the Romans (Isa. 53:3, Mark 15:13-32)
- Piercing (Ps. 22:16, Zech. 12:10, John 19:34-37)
- Burial (Isa. 53:9, Matt. 27:57-60)

The likelihood that any random person could have fulfilled even just these eight Messianic prophecies is astonishingly small (1 in 10^{17}), and the probability that some random person might have fulfilled 48 of the major prophecies is vanishingly minute (1 in 10^{157}!).[239] Regarding the eight critical prophecies, they were "either given by inspiration of God or the prophets just wrote them as they thought they should be. In such a case, the prophets had just one chance in 10^{17} of having them come true in any man, but they all came true in Christ."[240] The odds overwhelmingly favor superintendence by God.

Consistent Testimony of Jesus's Followers

Jesus's followers had become so convinced of the truth of His claims that they carefully documented His life, death, and resurrection. They wanted people who had never seen Jesus to read about and believe in Him as their Redeemer and Messiah.[241] It would have been surprising if the new Jewish and Gentile believers (the first Christians) had not documented His life and explained how they understood Jesus to be their long-awaited Messiah.

Just as He prophesied about Himself, Jesus suffered at the hands of His own people; He was rejected, betrayed, crucified, died, and then was raised from the dead on the third day. How could He have correctly predicted the form His life would take apart from Divine inspiration, especially events that depended on the actions of people other than Himself?

When John's disciples asked Jesus if He was the expected Messiah, Jesus responded, "Go and tell John what you have seen and heard: the blind receive their sight, the lame walk, lepers are cleansed, and the deaf hear, the dead are raised up, the poor have good news preached to them."[242] Even the Jewish leadership who refused to accept Him as their Messiah witnessed the miracles performed by Him and indirectly testified to their authenticity.[243]

Jesus's Death Confirmed

Jesus died on the cross. The Roman guards knew how to crucify, and they knew how to tell if a person was dead. But even if initially there might have been some doubt, it was removed when the soldier sent to break the legs of those being crucified thrust his spear into Jesus's side.[244] The outflow of blood and "water" (pericardial fluid) indicated that the spear pierced the pericardium and the heart itself, which would have killed Jesus if He had not been already dead.

The Consequences Surrounding Jesus's Missing Body

Knowing about Jesus's teaching that He would rise from the dead on the third day, the Jewish religious leaders asked Pilate for a guard to be set at the tomb; they feared that Jesus's disciples might steal the body and then proclaim His resurrection.[245] But somehow the tomb was empty, and the disciples were told that Jesus had risen. Even the bribery of the guards at the tomb lent credence to the Resurrection; the Roman guards would never have let anyone past them, nor would they have forsaken their post. To do so would have been to invite their execution as punishment.[246] Something had to have happened that could not be explained by common fishermen overpowering the armed and experienced Roman guards, rolling away the stone covering the tomb, and then stealing the body. Even if the body had been stolen, the guards and religious leaders could have followed the thieves, found it, and proved the Resurrection to be false.[247]

The Resurrected Jesus Appearing in the Flesh

Immediately after His resurrection, Jesus greeted individual disciples, and they worshipped Him. On other occasions, Jesus somehow appeared to all His disciples *without coming through the locked door*, spoke and ate with them, allowed them to see and touch Him and His wounds, and even accepted their worship; Jesus made it clear that He was real, not an apparition of some kind.[248]

As Jesus met with His disciples over the forty days following His resurrection, He explained how the Hebrew Scriptures testify to Him, and He commissioned the disciples to be His witnesses to the whole world once the promised Holy Spirit came to empower them. The forty days ended with Jesus's ascension to Heaven.[249]

The Arrival of the Holy Spirit—and the Effects on the Early Church

Upon the outpouring of the Holy Spirit at Pentecost—fifty days after Jesus's resurrection, the disciples were transformed from fearful, often-foolish, common men into bold apostles able to stand before the same crowds who called for Jesus's crucifixion as well as the Jewish religious leaders in order to proclaim the Resurrection of Jesus in spite of the threat of serious punishment, including death. Traditionally, it is believed that all but one of the twelve apostles were eventually martyred for their beliefs. We know that the Apostle

James, the brother of John, was the first apostle to die, killed by Herod. The Apostle John spent the last years of his life in exile on the island of Patmos, where he wrote his Gospel and three letters to the church.[250]

The emboldened apostles—indeed, all Christ followers—were also empowered by the Holy Spirit to heal in the name of Jesus. So well-attested was the healing of a man who was lame from birth that even the Jewish ruling council could not deny that a remarkable sign had been performed by the apostles and was evident to all the inhabitants of Jerusalem. Acts 5:12 tells us that many signs and wonders were regularly performed among the people by the hands of the apostles. Those witnessed in Acts included the healing of a man who had been bedridden for eight years, the raising of Dorcas and Eutychus from the dead, the healing of a cripple, the casting out of a demon, and the healing of a ruler's father.[251]

The immediate birth and growth of the Christian church on the Day of Pentecost—among the very people who had demanded the Crucifixion of Jesus—was a witness to the truth of what was preached and to the power of the Holy Spirit to convict and change hearts. Three thousand people were added to the community of believers at the preaching of Peter on the Day of Pentecost, and "the Lord added to their number day by day those who were being saved."[252]

Converted by a vision of the resurrected living Jesus, the zealous Pharisee Saul/Paul was transformed from being the early Christian church's worst persecutor into one of the greatest of the apostles. Though he suffered countless trials and was ultimately martyred for his faith, Paul brought the Gospel to the entire Gentile world—the Roman Empire.[253]

Extra-Biblical Sources

In addition to the witness of Scripture to the Resurrection, we also have extra-biblical testimony:

- The first century Roman historian, Tacitus (AD 56-120), documented the torture of hated Christians by the Emperor Nero for their belief in "Christus, from whom the name had its origin, [and who] suffered the extreme penalty ... at the hands of Pontius Pilatus, [which checked] a most mischievous superstition," likely the Resurrection.[254]
- Suetonius (AD 69-122), the chief secretary to Emperor Hadrian, also wrote of Christians being punished as "a body of people addicted to a novel and mischievous superstition."[255]
- While there is some question as to the extent of the original wording, the Jewish historian Josephus (AD 37-100) wrote—at a minimum—that Jesus was a wise (or virtuous) man who was condemned to be crucified by Pilate; further, His disciples continued to follow Him and to proclaim that He was alive and had appeared to them three days after His crucifixion.[256]
- Pliny the Younger (AD 61-113), Roman author and administrator, wrote about Christian worship practices, that "they were in the habit of meeting on a certain fixed day before it was light, when they sang in alternate verses a hymn to Christ, as to a god."[257]

This represents only some of the evidence for the truth of the Resurrection; other academic scholars provide additional arguments and dive deeper into the historical truth of the Resurrection. For recommended reading, see William Lane Craig's *On Guard* or Josh McDowell's *The New Evidence That Demands a Verdict*.

The Resurrection is key to accepting the truth of the Bible. If Jesus is raised from the dead as He said, then all that He said and did is validated as *the* truth about humankind, about Himself, about God the Father, and about the Holy Spirit.

12
Conclusion

> "You never know how much you really
> believe anything until its truth or
> falsehood becomes a matter of life and
> death to you."[258]
> C.S. Lewis, *A Grief Observed*

We have come a long way from where we began: Pilate dismissively asking Jesus, "What is truth?"

Defining truth as "that which corresponds to reality," we set out on a search to know more about reality, and we found that we were able to talk about certain facets of reality as if what we were saying was actually true, not just for me or you, but true for *all people* at *all times*, whether we believe it or not.

We also recognized, however, that we live within the reality we seek to understand, so observing reality from within, we can never quite grasp its whole in order to properly piece together those parts we do know (or think we know) about it. It became clear that if we are ever to fully know the truth about reality and the answers to our most pressing questions, then we need a "Someone" from "outside" or apart from our world to fill in our gaps of understanding.

In our search for that "Someone," we concluded that it is more plausible than not that the God who is "an uncaused, unembodied Mind who transcends the physical universe and even space and time themselves" had created this world and all living things,[259] and that He alone could satisfy our need to understand it; only He would know all there is to know about reality.

Having established that it is reasonable to think that this God could communicate with human beings, we then asked whether He has told us anything about what He knows, focusing on the Bible as a plausible source of God-speech.

But does the Bible address the pressing questions that we have? The following summarizes its answers:

1. How did we get here?

We were created by God, in His image and likeness.[260]

2. What is our purpose?

We were made to have fellowship with God and to be stewards over His creation.[261]

3. Is the God of the Hebrew Scriptures angry and vindictive?

- The God of the Hebrew Scriptures does not tolerate rebellion against Him, but He judges with righteous judgment those who sin (Gen. 18:25, Deut. 16:18-20, Ps. 96:13).

- He is not vindictive but judges according to His perfect moral character (Num. 23:19, Ps. 75:6-10, Ps. 98:9).

- His anger is a proper response to sin, to that which mars the perfection of His creation and especially His creatures—men and women—made in His image and likeness (Gen. 3:14-19, Ps. 78).

- In fact, the promises of the Saving Messiah are all given by the God of the Hebrew Scriptures, beginning with the judgment of the Serpent who deceived Adam and Eve (Gen. 3:15). He declares Himself to be merciful, "[keeping] covenant and steadfast love with those who love him and keep his commandments, to a thousand generations" (Deut. 7:9, Ps. 116:5).

- The true character of God is revealed in His Son, Jesus. God so loved the world—His creation, including all the people in it—that He gave His Son, Jesus, for us as our Messiah (or Christ), our Savior and Redeemer who died for our sins.[262]

4. **Why is there so much evil in this world?**

- From the first rebellion of Adam and Eve, all human beings have rebelled and continue to rebel against God, not desiring God's will but their own.[263]
- All human beings have been separated from fellowship with God due to their rebellion against Him.[264]

5. **Does God love me?**

- Yes! God knew we would be rebellious and selfish, so He sent Jesus to destroy the enemy of humanity, even to His own hurt, to save us.[265]
- John 15:13 tells us, "Greater love has no one than this, that someone lay down his life for his friends." Jesus laid down his life for us.

6. **If God loves us, why doesn't He automatically forgive everyone?**

There is a sense by which God does provide for "automatic" forgiveness for all people: Every person who places their trust in Jesus as their Lord and Savior are forgiven apart from any further action on their part. We are born into a broken relationship with God and a tendency to rebel against Him in our thoughts, words, and deeds. Only Divine action—that of the substitutionary sacrifice of Jesus Christ—can forgive and restore our spiritual connection to God as our Father.

> For God so loved the world, that he gave his only Son, that whoever believes in him should not perish but have eternal life. For God did not send his Son into the world to condemn the world, but in order that the world might be saved through him. Whoever believes in him is not condemned, but whoever does not believe is condemned already, because he has not believed in the name of the only Son of God.[266]

So, all people are freely given the opportunity to place their faith in Jesus Christ; He is God's gift to the world. To receive Him is to place oneself in the very center of God's will, but to reject Jesus is to continue in a state of rebellion against His Father.

7. **What does it mean to be saved?**

- Acts 4:12 tells us that "there is salvation in no one else, for there is no other name under heaven given among men by which we must be saved." To those who believe in Jesus Christ as their Lord and Savior, they are given the Holy Spirit to guide them, to change their hearts to desire to do what God requires. Indeed, the people who put their faith in Jesus and receive His Holy Spirit are transformed to live a new life that pleases God, their Heavenly Father.[267]
- Those who believe receive forgiveness of their sins (their rebellion against God), are incorporated into the family of God ("the church"), and receive the promise of eternal life with God, with a resurrected body and soul.

8. **What happens after I die?**

- Upon death, we will be judged (Heb. 9:27), but those who die in Christ will be saved; they will be raised to heaven where we will receive a new glorified body and be forever with Him (1 Cor. 15:36-49, Rev. 21:3-4).
- Those who die apart from Christ will suffer eternal judgment (Rev. 20:12-15).

The Bible gives us plausible answers to the questions that plague all humankind, but is it more plausibly true than not that the answers given in the Bible come from the God who created our world and us?

While there are objections to the answers given in the Bible, there is no other document that provides entirely coherent answers to the questions we have about this world and our place in it. Have we eliminated all doubt and answered all the questions that could be asked? No. Instead, believing it is truthful, we have allowed the Bible to speak for itself.

What is truth, Pilate?

Jesus stood there with you, but you refused to see in Him the essence—the very source—of all reality, the Truth embodied in the

Son of God.[268] *He* is God's answer to the most important questions that face every human being.

There will always be unanswered questions in this life, whether we place our faith in Christ or not. But we have now been introduced to *the* Truth, as was Pilate.

Pilate sent Him to be crucified.

What will you do with Him?

Appendix A
The Evolution of Darwinism

In his book *On the Origin of Species by Means of Natural Selection,* first published in 1859, Charles Darwin set forth his theory of evolution of all life, assuming the prior existence of one or a few organisms as a given.[269] Although he allowed for the possibility that those original organisms may have been created, we know from other sources that he speculated about the possibility of life itself arising naturally.[270] Other evolutionists ultimately theorized that very thing, incorporating origin-of-life studies (abiogenesis) under the umbrella of evolution.[271]

It was during the 1800s that several people began to think in evolutionary terms, but Darwin is credited with having identified a mechanism, "natural selection," by which biological change could be preserved, resulting in new varieties of organisms. Living things have various capacities and techniques for defending themselves from danger and competing for the resources they need to flourish; those organisms best able to do so are said to be "selected" for survival. Of course, nature does not actually choose one organism over another like we choose to befriend this person but not that person. Natural selection is just a pithy name for Darwin's observation that the organisms most fit for the environment where they live always win out in the survival game over the less fit. The fittest organisms survive long enough to reproduce and reproduce sufficiently well to overcome the death rate. Thus, *natural selection is an effect, not a cause.* It is only *after* an organism changes and reproduces that natural selection can be observed, preserving offspring that are more survivable than organisms that have not changed.

But what led Darwin to think that whole new body functions and structures could develop from simple life forms? Until Charles Lyell proposed his theory of uniformitarianism, which asserts that all natural processes have continued without change since the inception of the earth, it was thought that the earth was only six thousand to twelve thousand years old, an insufficient amount of time for a slow process like natural selection to produce significant changes in any living thing. With the publication of Lyell's theory, however, scientists began to think that the earth could be vastly older by millions of years.[272] Accordingly, Darwin envisioned the possibility that natural selection might be sufficient to enact major biological changes through the accumulation of an uncountable number of minor changes, gradually transforming existing life forms into entirely new ones over those extended periods of time.[273] We need to keep in mind that Darwin did not have our current understanding of genetics. No one in his day had any concept of the complexity of the cell or the mechanism by which genetic traits were passed from one generation to the next. Consequently, Darwin had no reason (from a genetic standpoint, at least) to doubt that natural selection could eventually "breed" any and every kind of life form.

Furthermore, an abundance of fossils was discovered during the late 18th and early 19th centuries, having been exposed during the Industrial Revolution as companies dug for coal in support of the every-increasing energy demands of their factories.[274] While some scientists believed that the fossils were the result of one or multiple catastrophic events (such as the biblical Flood) many were coming to believe that they had accumulated over long periods of time, consistent with Lyell's uniformitarian theory of geology. It was not unreasonable for Darwin and others to wonder if there had been some natural process at work, slowly transforming existing life into newer, more complex life forms. Ultimately, Darwin proposed natural selection as the mechanism to explain life's gradual development, thinking his explanation to be largely, although not entirely, consistent with the fossil record and the presumed time available to accomplish the evolutionary development of some species.[275]

Again, natural selection does not cause anything; it is a description of nature's working *after* a change has already taken place. So, Darwin needed to explain how changes could arise in the first place, changes that natural selection would then act upon. It was not until scientists came to understand the genetic makeup of life that they believed they had found their answer. While different combinations of inherited genetic characteristics can affect how well-suited people and other living things are to their environments, variations of this sort are part of an organism's essential nature. As scientists gained greater understanding of genetic inheritance, however, they began to wonder whether an organism's genetic code (DNA) might be susceptible to *radical* alteration as a consequence of genetic *mutations*—random mistakes or other corruptions to the normal functioning of a cell.[276] As you might suspect, given that mutations are *mistakes*, most of them are bad; on occasion, however, they can be non-harmful or even beneficial,[277] and scientists knew that many plant and animal varieties were the product of non-harmful genetic mutations that had become permanent adaptations.[278] It was not a big leap, then, for scientists to imagine that the extent of genetic change might be unlimited. Consequently, they theorized that the DNA instructions of an organism could be wholly modified by the gradual accumulation of naturally selected beneficial genetic mutations, resulting in entirely new creatures.[279]

But theorizing that something might happen is not the same as demonstrating that it can or has happened. As I have shown, while microevolution is known for a fact, Darwinian evolution remains a questionable theory.

Appendix B
A Brief Review of Genetics

Biologists now know that every cell is like a miniature city with a control center, the nucleus, which we can think of as the city mayor. The mayor coordinates the city's separate functions, functions in a cell that are not unlike a city's workers, highway systems, boundaries, lawns and parks, post office, energy plants, waste disposal and recycling, and warehouses.[280] And the DNA molecule residing in the nucleus of every cell is like the city manager's office, maintaining the legal code and operating procedures, which advise the mayor what kind of city he is running, govern permissible actions, and direct accomplishing tasks.[281]

But what is DNA? For a more in-depth exploration of the topic, you can learn the basics online or from any introductory biology text.[282] Nonetheless, we can see from the depiction of a DNA fragment (below) that it has a very particular structure called a "double helix." Although it can vary greatly in length, the general structure of DNA is the same for every organism, providing the supporting framework for multitudes of "base pair" molecules, each rung in the figure representing a base pair. There are only four possible pairings—A-T, T-A, C-G, and G-C for short—but they can be used over and over again in different combinations in the same DNA.[283] In fact, the shortest DNA—that of a bacterium—contains some 160,000 base pairs, while the DNA of humans is more than 6.4 billion base pairs long.[284] While length provides a clue as to the complexity of an organism, the base pairs used and their order are what determines its *genetic makeup*—the instructions or coding for an organism's development and functioning (like a computer program). Slight differences in the base pair sequences of two humans, for example, can cause one to have brown eyes and the other to have blue eyes, even though they have DNA of the same length. As a more striking example, humans and mice apparently have DNA of a similar length but are clearly *not* very much alike![285]

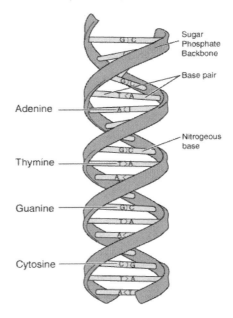

Sugar
Phosphate
Backbone

Base pair

Adenine

Nitrogeous
base

Thymine

Guanine

Cytosine

Figure A-1: Sample DNA Fragment[286]

Regarding the kinds of instructions, think of a DNA base pair as an English word. If you have (or have had) children in your home, then you have used the commands, "Get up" and "Go to bed." One command or instruction requires two words, while the other one requires three, but the length of each instruction indicates nothing about its meaning or importance. Similarly, the *number of base pairs* required to define an instruction provides no clue as to its significance or purpose. The same can be said of the *number of instructions*. For example, a computer program is an ordered collection of commands, each one chosen from a specific set of commands—the "programming language"—that a computer's operating system (the control center) can interpret. The greater the number of instructions, the larger the program and the more numerous or complex are the functions that the program has to perform, generally speaking. But two programs of comparable size may have completely different purposes and functions, such as is the case with Microsoft Word and Microsoft Excel. Microsoft Word was developed to compose heavily textual documents like this book, whereas Microsoft Excel was made for crunching numbers the way accountants do. Microsoft Word does not really know what to do with numbers, and Excel is confused by words, but both perform tasks that require extensive programming. Likewise, humans and mice have few things in common but are the result of a similar number of DNA instructions. The specific instructions used *and* their order—the genetic makeup—determine the job a program will accomplish or the kind of organism DNA will generate.

Appendix C
Evaluation Criteria and the Bible

The following are evaluation criteria for a writing claiming to contain God-speech as well as examples demonstrating that the Bible meets those criteria:

I.   Proper Credentials

    A.   Divine Authority

        1.   The creation account demonstrates that when God speaks, what He commands happens. Gen. 1:3, 6, 9, 11, 14, 20, 24, and 26 all show that God-speech is sufficient to cause that which He commands.

        2.   God gives the Ten Commandments in Exodus 20:1-17.

        3.   God has authority over all nations. In Jer. 1:9-10, God says to Jeremiah, the prophet, "Behold, I have put my words in your mouth. See, I have set you this day over nations and over kingdoms, to pluck up and to break down, to destroy and to overthrow, to build and to plant."

        4.   See Appendix D: The Gospels' Description of Jesus, for evidence of Jesus's Divine authority. For example, we read in John 14:6 that Jesus responds to Thomas, saying, "I am the way, and the truth, and the life. No one comes to the Father except through me."

    B.   Divine Identity

        1.   When Moses asks what He should be called, God tells him:

> I AM WHO I AM. *And He said, "Say this to the people of Israel:* I AM *has sent me to you." God also said to Moses, "Say this to the people of Israel: The Lord (that is, Yahweh or YHWH), the God of your fathers, the God of Abraham, the God of Isaac, and the God of Jaco*b, has sent me to you. This is my name forever, and thus I am to be remembered throughout all generations." (Exod. 3:14-15)

        2.   Using a Logos search[287] with the criteria "I am God" or "I am the Lord," we find that God identifies Himself at least 197 times in the Hebrew Scriptures. For example, in Gen. 17:1-2,

God says to Abram (later renamed Abraham), "I am God Almighty; walk before me, and be blameless, that I may make my covenant between me and you and may multiply you greatly."

3. More generally, by various names, God is identified as the speaker 13,670 times in the Hebrew Scriptures and an additional 117 times in the New Testament (based on the Logos search criterion, "speaker:person:God").

4. See Appendix D: The Gospels' Description of Jesus, for evidence of Jesus's names. For instance, in Luke 1:31 the angel Gabriel says to Mary, "And behold, you will conceive in your womb and bear a son, and you shall call His name Jesus."

C. Divine Personhood

1. The true God often identifies Himself as the One who brought the nation of Israel out of Egypt, or by His other actions on their behalf. For example, we read in Lev. 25:38, "I am the Lord your God, who brought you out of the land of Egypt to give you the land of Canaan, and to be your God."

2. Further, God often characterizes Himself in the Hebrew Scriptures in opposition to idols, as in Ps. 135:15-17:

3. The idols of the nations are silver and gold, the work of human hands. They have mouths, but do not speak; they have eyes, but do not see; they have ears, but do not hear, nor is there any breath in their mouths.

4. The following are examples of the goodness and righteousness of God:

   a) "For the Lord is righteous; He loves righteous deeds; the upright shall behold His face." (Ps. 11:7)

   b) Truly God is good to Israel, to those who are pure in heart." (Ps. 73:1)

   c) "Righteous are you, O Lord, and right are your rules. You have appointed your testimonies in righteousness and in all faithfulness." (Ps. 119:137-138)

   d) "Oh give thanks to the Lord, for He is good; for His steadfast love endures forever!" (1 Chron. 16:34)

Appendix C: Evaluation Criteria and the Bible

e) See Appendix D: The Gospels' Description of Jesus, for evidence that Jesus uniquely identifies Himself. As an example, in John 14:11 Jesus tells His disciples, "Believe me that I am in the Father and the Father is in me, or else believe on account of the works themselves."

II. Intimate Knowledge of Human Nature

A. God tells us in Gen. 1:26 that we were to be stewards of His creation, saying,

> Let us make man in our image, after our likeness. And let them have dominion over the fish of the sea and over the birds of the heavens and over the livestock and over all the earth and over every creeping thing that creeps on the earth.

B. God understands and responds to the needs of His people, saying in Isa. 43:1, "But now thus says the Lord, He who created you, O Jacob, He who formed you, O Israel: 'Fear not, for I have redeemed you; I have called you by name, you are mine.'"

C. Ps. 14:2-3 declares God's knowledge of human shortcomings:

> The Lord looks down from heaven on the children of man, to see if there are any who understand, who seek after God. They have all turned aside; together they have become corrupt; there is none who does good, not even one.

D. The Sermon of the Mount in Matthew chapters 5-7 demonstrates Jesus's Divine knowledge of human nature, as well as His own righteousness and authority to judge.

III. Rationally Truthful

A. The creation account is a sober description of the creation of the world and all living beings (Gen. 1:1–2:3).

B. "O Lord, who shall sojourn in your tent? Who shall dwell on your holy hill? He who walks blamelessly and does what is right and speaks truth in his heart." (Ps. 15:1-2)

C. "Hear, for I will speak noble things, and from my lips will come what is right, for my mouth will utter truth; wickedness is an abomination to my lips. All the words of my mouth are righteous; there is nothing twisted or crooked in them. They are all straight to

him who understands, and right to those who find knowledge."
(Prov. 8:6-9)

D. "Come now, let us reason together, says the Lord: though your sins
are like scarlet, they shall be as white as snow; though they are red
like crimson, they shall become like wool." (Isa. 1:18)

E. Isa. 44:9-20 provides a rational explanation of the folly of idolatry.

F. "I the LORD speak the truth; I declare what is right." (Isa. 45:19b)

G. See Appendix D: The Gospels' Description of Jesus, for evidence
that Jesus is rationally truthful. For example, we read in John 1:14
that John testifies about Jesus, saying, "And the Word became flesh
and dwelt among us, and we have seen His glory, glory as of the
only Son from the Father, full of grace and truth."

IV. Accommodated to Humanity

A. Rather than identify specific verses, we can observe God's
accommodation in the way He introduces the means of salvation to
Israel. First, God promises that the offspring of Eve will crush the
serpent; later, Abraham is chosen to bless the world; and then,
Israel is birthed, and Moses is raised up as its leader. As Israel
becomes a kingdom, we begin to understand that Messiah will be a
king and will be Someone with Divine authority. Each stage is
intended to lead Israel to a more mature understanding of the
coming Redeemer.

B. Finally, God sends Jesus, who fulfills the promises of the Hebrew
Scriptures and brings a fullness of understanding to God's people,
yet to be completed when Jesus returns.

V. Historically and Archaeologically Accurate

A. Accuracy

1. The Bible has gained a reputation of having accurately
recorded historical events, cultural markers, and the locations
of ancient cities and towns.[288] In particular, "The consensus
among contemporary scholars is that Luke ... is indeed a
careful, reliable recorder of history."[289]

B. Effects on People

1. When God made the Israelites "[His] people" (Exod. 3:7), He
gave them the Ten Commandments (Exod. 20:1-17) and the

Levitical laws that molded their lives by teaching them of their place and purpose in this world.

2. The New Testament teachings about Jesus transformed the lives, not only of the early Jewish believers, but also ultimately much of the world as Christian beliefs spread.

C. Supernatural Witness

1. God's prophet Elijah supernaturally defeated the prophets of Baal on Mount Carmel, demonstrating that Yahweh is the One true God, and showing that God does intervene in the affairs of humanity (1 Kings 18:20-40).

2. During His life, Jesus performed many miraculous signs (see Appendix D: The Gospels' Description of Jesus). The Resurrection is, no doubt, the most dramatic example of God's intervening in our world.

D. Prophecy

1. The clearest examples of fulfilled prophecies are those in the Hebrew Scriptures that are fulfilled in Jesus Christ.[290]

Appendix D
The Gospels' Description of Jesus

This appendix describes Jesus's human, Divine, and human-Divine (or "dual") characteristics, as well as assertions about His role in humanity's salvation.[291] Each subsection is further divided according to the character(s) to whom the testimony is attributed, including a list of supporting Bible passages. Where it seems clear, references to the same event are included from each of the Gospels as evidence of a common understanding and belief among the Gospel authors.

EXAMPLES OF JESUS'S HUMAN NATURE

1. **The Gospel narratives' attribution of human characteristics to Jesus:**

    - Mary gave birth to Jesus as a baby (Luke 2:7, 2:12, 2:16; Matt. 1:16, 1:25)
    - Jesus was a normal (albeit intelligent) boy who grew to adulthood in His parents' household (Luke 2:41-52)
    - Jesus lived in Nazareth and was called a Nazarene (Matt. 2:23)
    - Jesus exhibited normal human emotions, such as mercy, anger, joy, agony, fear, concern, humor, and compassion (Matt. 9:27-30; Mark 3:5; Luke 10:21, 22:44; John 11:33, 11:35, 11:38)

2. **Statements by Gospel characters regarding Jesus's human nature:**

    - Angel Gabriel to Mary:
        o You will give birth to a son, who you are to name Jesus (Luke 1:31)
        o Your son will be given the throne of David (possibly a reference to Jesus's Divine authority when coupled with v. 33, but Mary would have understood it—at least in part—as a reference to the earthly kingdom) (Luke 1:32)
    - Angel of the Lord to Joseph:
        o Mary will give birth to a son (Matt. 1:21)
        o Directs Joseph how to protect the child (Matt. 2:13-15, 2:19-21)
    - Townspeople know Jesus as Joseph's son (Luke 4:22)

- Nathanael refers to Jesus as "Rabbi" and calls Him "the King of Israel" (possibly a reference to Jesus's Divine nature since Nathanael also calls Jesus "the Son of God") (John 1:49)
- The crowds call Jesus "a king," seemingly as an earthly title (the Jewish people were looking for a Messiah who would be their earthly king to re-establish the Davidic kingdom[292]) (Luke 19:38)
- Disciples and others call Jesus, "Lord" as a human title of respect equivalent to the English Sir or Mr.[293] (Matt. 8:6; Mark 7:28)
- Disciples call Jesus "Master"[294] (Luke 5:5, 8:24, 8:45, 9:33, 9:49, 17:13)
- Disciples call Jesus "Rabbi," that is, "Teacher" (John 1:38)

3. **Statements Jesus made about Himself that suggest His human nature:**

- Seeks God's will, not His own (John 5:30)
- Puts Himself in the place of all human beings (Matt. 4:1-11)

4. **Things Jesus did (or were done to Him) that would be expected of His human nature:**

- Feels temptations of hunger, thirst, power, and fear of suffering and death (Luke 4:1-13, 22:41-44)
- Teaches in the Jewish synagogues (Luke 4:15)
- Cries over the death of His friend, Lazarus (John 11:35)
- Makes provision for His mother's welfare (John 19:26-27)

EXAMPLES OF JESUS'S DIVINE NATURE

5. **According to the Gospel writers:**

- He existed and was with God before the world came into being, but "distinct from" God (God the Father, by implication) (John 1:1-2)
- He is God, the Word, the fullness of the expression of God's being from the beginning (before the creation of the world) (John 1:1)
- He is God, the Word, the Creator of the world, and made everything that has ever been made (John 1:3)
- As God, the Word, He has (all) life in Himself, and His life gives light (truth) to humanity (John 1:4)
- He is referred to as "the Lord Jesus" (Mark 16:19-20; Luke 24:3)

- As "the only God, who is at the Father's side," Jesus reveals the Father (John 1:18)
- He is called the Son of God (Mark 1:1)
- He is called "the Christ, the Son of God" and the source of life through faith in His name (John 20:31)

6. **Claims Jesus made about Himself pertaining to His Divine nature:**

- He was given all authority in heaven and on Earth (Matt. 28:18)
- He is descended from (that is, came from) heaven (John 3:13)
- He is eternal ("I am") (John 8:56-59)
- He had authority on Earth to forgive sins (Matt. 9:1-8; Mark 2:3-12; Luke 5:17-26)
- He was with God the Father before the world existed (John 17:5)
- He gives life to people as He wills (John 4:13-14, 5:21, 6:27-51, 10:27-28, 17:1-2)
- He would give His own life as a ransom for many (Matt. 20:28; Mark 10:45; John 10:15-17)
- He would willingly give up His life in death (Luke 23:46)
- He will judge the world (Matt. 19:28-30; Luke 12:49-53; John 5:21-24, 8:21-26, 9:39)
- He has life in Himself (John 5:26, 11:25, 15:1-2)
- He is the light of the world (John 8:12, 9:5)
- He is the Lord of the Sabbath (Matt. 12:8; Mark 2:28; Luke 6:5)
- He made Himself equal with God by claiming God as His Father (John 5:18)
- He is one with the Father (John 10:30, 12:44-45, 14:10-11)
- He has overcome the world (John 16:33)
- He is the One prophesied by Moses (John 5:46)
- He prophesied His own suffering, resurrection, and/or raising of Himself (Matt. 17:9-12, 17:22-23, 26:30-32; Luke 9:21-22, 18:31-33)
- He reveals the Father (Matt. 11:27; Luke 10:22; John 14:7-9)
- He teaches so that His hearers might be saved (John 5:34)
- He teaches that salvation is through Him (Matt. 10:16-23, 16:24-28; Mark 8:34-38, 13:9-13; Luke 7:36-50, 19:1-10; John 3:16-17, 7:37-39, 10:7-18)
- He fulfills the Law (Matt. 5:17-20, 21:42, 26:54-56; Mark 12:10; Luke 24:25-27, 24:44-48; John 5:39, 10:31-39, 15:25)
- He deserves the same honor as the Father (John 5:23)

FOR THE LOVE OF TRUTH

- He refers to Himself as the Son of Man, in a way that suggests that He is the "Son of Man" of Daniel 7:13, the One who is given everlasting dominion (Matt. 9:6, 16:13-17, 26:64; Mark 8:38, 14:21, 14:62; Luke 9:22, 9:58, 22:69; John 1:51, 3:13, 8:28). Per Table 1, below, there are 74 verses in which Jesus is referred to as the Son of Man

- He refers to Himself as the Son of God, either directly or by inference (confirming what the religious leaders accuse Him of) (Matt. 26:63, 27:43; Luke 22:70-71; John 3:18, 5:25, 10:36, 11:4). Per Table 1, below, there are 25 verses in which Jesus is referred to as the Son of God

- He is the source of eternal life (John 3:14-15, John 5:21, John 6:40, John 6:51-58, John 10:27-28, John 11:25-26, John 17:1-2)

- He is the Good Shepherd (John 10:11-14)

- He is the way (to the Father), the truth, and the life (John 14:6-7)

- His works bear witness of being sent by the Father (John 5:36)

- He refers to Himself as the Messiah (Christ), either directly or by inference (confirming what the religious leaders accuse Him of) (Matt. 23:10; Mark 8:29-30, 14:61-62; Luke 9:20-21, 22:67-71; John 4:25-26, 17:3)

- He preaches the good news of the Kingdom of God (Luke 4:18-19, 4:43, 7:22)

- He is without sin (John 8:46)

- He promises to send the Holy Spirit and to remain with the disciples always (through the Holy Spirit) (Matt. 28:20; John 14:15-18)

- He gives authority to His disciples "over unclean spirits, to cast them out, and to heal every disease and every affliction" (Matt. 10:1)

7. **Things Jesus *did* (or that were done to Him) that reveal His Divine nature:**

- Miracles that reveal His authority over the physical world:

  o Turns water to wine (John 2:1-11)
  o Directs large catch of fish (Luke 5:1-11)
  o Calms a storm (Matt. 8:23-27; Mark 4:35-41; Luke 8:22-25)
  o Feeds the 5,000 (Matt. 14:13-21; Mark 6:30-44; Luke 9:10-17; John 6:1-15)
  o Walks on water (Matt. 14:22-33; Mark 6:45-52; John 6:16-21)

180

- ○ Feeds the 4,000 (Matt. 15:32-39; Mark 8:1-9)
- ○ Directs catch of fish to pay Temple tax (Matt. 17:24-27)
- ○ Curses a fig tree (Matt. 21:18-22; Mark 11:12-14, 11:20-23)
- Healings of physical disabilities (not including the raising of the dead and His own resurrection), revealing His authority over the human body, such as:
  - ○ Many with varying physical issues (Matt. 15:29-31, 21:14; Luke 7:21-22)
  - ○ The blind and lame (Matt. 9:27-30, 20:29-34; Mark 8:22-26, 10:46-52; Luke 18:35-43; John 9:1-11)
  - ○ The servant's ear (Luke 22:47-51)
  - ○ The man with the withered hand (Matt. 12:10-13; Mark 3:1-5; Luke 6:6-10)
  - ○ A paralytic (Matt. 9:1-8; Mark 2:1-12; Luke 5:17-26; John 5:2-15)
  - ○ A woman with a flow of blood (Matt. 9:20-22; Mark 5:25-34; Luke 8:43-48)
  - ○ The deaf man (Mark 7:31-35)
  - ○ The infirm woman (Luke 13:10-13)
  - ○ The Centurion's paralyzed servant (Matt. 8:5-13; Luke 7:2-10)
- Healings of diseases, revealing His authority over human illnesses, such as:
  - ○ The multitudes (Matt. 4:23, 8:16-17, 9:35, 12:15, 14:13-14, 14:34-36, 15:29-31, 19:1-2; Mark 1:32-34, 3:9-10, 6:5, 6:54-56; Luke 4:40, 5:15, 6:19, 7:21-22, 9:11; John 6:2)
  - ○ Leprosy (Matt. 8:1-3; Mark 1:40-42; Luke 5:12-13, 17:11-19)
  - ○ Fever (Matt. 8:14-15; Mark 1:30-31; Luke 4:38-39; John 4:46-53)
  - ○ Dropsy (Luke 14:1-4)
- Delivery from evil or unclean spirits, revealing His authority over the spiritual realm, such as:
  - ○ Many oppressed by demons (Matt. 8:16-17; Mark 1:32-34, 1:39, 3:11-12; Luke 4:41, 6:17-18, 7:21)
  - ○ Man/men with demons (Matt. 8:28-32; Mark 5:1-13; Luke 8:26-33)
  - ○ Man who was mute (Matt. 9:32-33)
  - ○ Man who was blind and mute (Matt. 12:22)
  - ○ Daughter of Canaanite woman (Matt. 15:21-28; Mark 7:24-30)
  - ○ Boy with seizures (Matt. 17:14-18; Mark 9:14-27)

- o   Man with unclean spirit in the synagogue (Mark 1:23-26; Luke 4:33-35)
- Raising the dead:
  - o   Jairus's daughter (Luke 8:40-42, 49-56; Matt. 9:18-19, 23-26; Mark 5:21-24, 35-43)
  - o   Widow's son (Luke 7:11-17)
  - o   Lazarus (John 11:1-44)
- Being taken into heaven (Luke 24:51; Mark 16:19)
- Being raised from the dead (Matt. 28:1-10; Mark 16:1-14; Luke 24:1-12; John 20:1-10)
- Appearing to His disciples after being raised (Matt. 28:16-20; Luke 24:13-35, 24:36-49; John 20:11-18, 20:19-23, 20:24-29, 21:1-14)

8. **Statements made by God the Father about Jesus's Divine nature:**

- Calls Jesus His Son, His chosen one (Luke 9:35)
- Calls Jesus His beloved Son (Matt. 3:17, 17:5; Mark 1:11, 9:7; Luke 3:22)

9. **Statements by various Gospel characters regarding Jesus's Divine nature:**

- Angel Gabriel tells Mary:
  - o   He will be called "Son of the Most High" (Luke 1:32)
  - o   He "will reign over the house of Jacob forever, and of his kingdom there will be no end" (Luke 1:32-33)
  - o   He will be called "holy—the Son of God" (Luke 1:35)
  - o   He will "save his people from their sins" (Matt. 1:18-25)
- Angels tell the shepherds of the birth of "a Savior, who is Christ the Lord" (Luke 2:11)
- Simeon tells Mary and Joseph that Jesus will be a "light for revelation to the Gentiles" (Luke 2:32)
- John the Baptist tells the disciples that Jesus:
  - o   Will baptize with the Holy Spirit and with fire (Matt. 3:11; Mark 1:8; Luke 3:16; John 1:33)
  - o   Is the "Lamb of God who takes away the sin of the world" (John 1:29, 1:36)
  - o   Is "the Son of God" (John 1:34)

- Philip declares to Nathanael, "We have found him of whom Moses in the Law and also the prophets wrote, Jesus of Nazareth, the son of Joseph" (John 1:45)
- Jesus's disciples and others call Jesus "Lord," suggesting a belief in Jesus's Divine lordship[295] (Matt. 17:4; Mark 7:28; Luke 5:8; John 6:68, 9:38)
- Jesus's disciples:
  - Call Jesus "Son of God" and "the Christ, the Son of the living God" (Matt. 14:33, 16:16; John 1:49, 11:27)
  - Worship Jesus (Matt. 14:33, 28:17; Luke 24:52)
  - Believe Jesus is the One promised by Moses in the Scriptures (John 1:45)
- Thomas declares, "My Lord and my God" (John 20:28)
- The woman at the well calls Jesus a prophet (John 4:19)
- The townspeople believe that Jesus is "the Savior of the world" (John 4:42)
- The people who witness the resurrection of the widow's son call Jesus a prophet (Luke 7:16)
- The Centurion at the cross calls Jesus the Son of God (Matt. 27:54; Mark 15:39)
- Nicodemus claims that Jesus is a teacher come from God (John 3:2)
- The Magi refer to Jesus as "he who has been born King of the Jews" (possibly a reference to Jesus's Divine nature since the Magi say they've come to worship Him) (Matt. 2:2)
- The man born blind worships Jesus (John 9:38)
- The blind men, by faith in Jesus, call Him the Son of David (Matt. 9:27)
- The Canaanite woman, by faith, calls Jesus the Son of David (Matt. 15:22)
- The religious leaders and others accuse Jesus of referring to Himself as equal to the Temple and having the ability to raise Himself (Matt. 26:61, 27:40; Mark 14:58, 15:29; John 2:18-22)
- Religious leaders and others tell Pilate that Jesus made Himself to be the Son of God (John 19:7)
- The demons call Jesus the:
  - Holy One of God (Mark 1:24; Luke 4:34)
  - Son of God (Matt. 8:29; Mark 3:11; Luke 4:41)
  - Son of the Most High God (Mark 5:7; Luke 8:28)

EXAMPLES OF JESUS'S DUAL NATURE

1. **The Gospel writers say:**

   - God, the Word, became a human being, the Son of God (John 1:14)
   - Jesus was filled with the power of the Spirit (Luke 4:14)
   - Jesus would fulfill the prophecy of Isaiah, that He would be called "'Immanuel' (which means, God with us)" (Matt. 1:23)

2. **An angel tells Mary that Jesus would be called the Son of God (Luke 1:35)**

3. **The Angel of the Lord tells Joseph that Jesus would save His people from their sins (Matt. 1:21)**

4. **The Magi refer to Jesus as "he who has been born King of the Jews" ("King of the Jews" seems a reference to Jesus's humanity), but also worship Him (Matt. 2:2, 2:11)**

THE WITNESS TO JESUS'S IDENTITY

Search Criteria	Number of Gospel References				
	Matthew	Mark	Luke	John	Total
"Jesus" AND "Lord" (Where Jesus is addressed as "Lord"	23	2	22	25	**72**
"Jesus" AND "Lord" (Where a narrator refers to Jesus as "Lord")	37	11	46	36	**130**
"Jesus" AND "Son of God"	8	3	5	9	**25**
"God" AND "Father"	4	1	5	7	**17**
"Jesus" AND "Father" OR "my Father"	49	12	28	91	**180**
"Jesus" AND "Christ" OR "Messiah"	4	2	4	4	**14**
"Jesus" AND "Son of Man"	28	11	24	11	**74**
"Jesus" AND "Teacher" OR "Rabbi"	8	14	12	9	**43**
"Jesus" AND "Savior" OR "Redeemer"	0	0	2	1	**3**

Table A-1. Frequency of Gospel References to Jesus's Identity in the Bible (English Standard Version)[296]

Search Criteria	Number of Non-Gospel References			
	Acts	Epistles	Revelation	Total
"Jesus" AND "Lord"	9	0	3	12
"Jesus" AND "Son of God"	1	16	1	18
"God" AND "Father"	1	1	0	2
"Jesus" AND ("Father" OR "my Father")	2	3	0	5
"Jesus" AND ("Christ" OR "Messiah")	0	0	0	0
"Jesus" AND "Son of Man"	0	0	0	0
"Jesus" AND ("Teacher" OR "Rabbi")	0	0	0	0
"Jesus" AND ("Savior" OR "Redeemer")	2	18	1	21
"Jesus" AND "Lord"	46	239	10	295

Table A-2. Frequency of Non-Gospel References to Jesus's Identity (English Standard Version)[297]

Appendix E
Trustworthiness of the New Testament

This appendix addresses the trustworthiness of the Bible's New Testament, whether the text we have today is a reliable transmission of the original writings of the apostles and other leaders of the first-century Christian church.

Even if we question the truth of the New Testament, we have good reason to trust that our modern Bible accurately represents what the New Testament authors actually wrote. With almost 5,700 copies in the original Greek language (and over 20,000 more in other languages) and a time gap of only 300 years between the most significant existing copies and the original source writings, no other ancient document has anything comparable to the volume of evidence we have for the accuracy of the New Testament.[298] For example, the greatest number of copies we have of any non-New Testament document (Homer's *Iliad*) is 643, with a 400-year time gap between the original and the earliest surviving copy, and yet scholars believe that our *Iliad* accurately represents the original manuscript.[299] With so many manuscript copies of the New Testament to compare against, scholars confidently identify and eliminate discrepancies between copies, minimizing the number and extent of questionable words or phrases.[300] Further, every other ancient writing that we accept as authentic has at least a 400-year time gap between the original and the existing copies, and most have time gaps greater than 1,000 years.[301]

The 300 years separating the original New Testament writings from the earliest existing copies, however, could still leave us skeptical of the accuracy of our current versions. But the length of the time gap is not as important as the care taken in copying the documents. The Hebrew Scriptures, for instance, were so carefully copied by scribes that the book of Isaiah in the Masoretic Text dating to about AD 916, is virtually identical to the Dead Sea Scroll of Isaiah, dating to approximately 125 BC, a time gap of more than 1,000 years.[302] The Masoretic Text of Isaiah contains no variations from the Isaiah Scroll that change the original meaning.[303] It is reasonable to expect that those who copied and passed along the New Testament manuscripts were as careful as those who copied the Hebrew Scriptures. While it is not possible to be 100 percent certain, the evidence suggests that it's more plausible than not that our present-day New Testament reliably records what was originally written about Jesus.

BIBLIOGRAPHY

"55 Old Testament Prophecies About Jesus." Jesus Film Project. A Cru Ministry, November 17, 2021. https://www.jesusfilm.org/blog/old-testament-prophecies.

"Genetics." *Learn.Genetics.* University of Utah, Accessed December 21, 2023. http://learn.genetics.utah.edu.

"Natural Selection." Oxford Languages and Google. Oxford University Press, Accessed May 13, 2023. https://www.google.com/search?q=natural+selection+definition&rlz=1C1CHBF_enUS943US943&oq=&aqs=chrome.0.69i59i450l8.266418379j0j15&sourceid=chrome&ie=UTF-8.

"Phylum." BiologyOnline. Accessed May 18, 2023. https://www.biologyonline.com/dictionary/phylum.

"Reasonable Doubt." 'Lectric Law Library Lexicon. Accessed June 2, 2022. https://www.lectlaw.com/def2/q016.htm.

"Size Matters: A Whole Genome Is 6.4B Letters." Veritas Genetics. Veritas Intercontinental, July 28, 2017. https://www.veritasgenetics.com/our-thinking/whole-story/.

"The Changing Global Religious Landscape." Pew Research Center. April 5, 2017. http://www.pewforum.org/2017/04/05/the-changing-global-religious-landscape/.

"The Global Religious Landscape." Pew Research Center. Pew Research Center, December 18, 2012. https://www.pewresearch.org/religion/2012/12/18/global-religious-landscape-exec/.

"The Science Behind the Human Genome Project." Human Genome Project Information. U.S. Department of Energy Office of Science, Office of Biological and Environmental Research, Human Genome Program, March 26, 2008. http://web.ornl.gov/sci/techresources/Human_Genome/project/info.shtml.

"Transitional Features." Understanding Evolution. University of California Museum of Paleontology, June 2020. http://evolution.berkeley.edu/evosite/lines/IAtransitional.shtml.

"Updates to the OED." *Oxford English Dictionary.* Oxford University Press, June 2020. https://www.oed.com/information/updates/.

"What Is a Mutation?" Learn.Genetics. University of Utah, Accessed May 12, 2023. https://learn.genetics.utah.edu/content/basics/mutation.

"Why Did Blood and Water Come Out of Jesus' Side when He Was Pierced?" Got Questions. Got Questions Ministries, Accessed February 6, 2023. https://www.gotquestions.org/blood-water-Jesus.html.

"World Languages." DayTranslations. Day Translations, Inc., Accessed July 18, 2018. https://www.daytranslations.com/world-languages.

Wikipedia. 2023. "The Kingdom of Speech." Wikimedia Foundation. Last modified March 14, 2023. https://en.wikipedia.org/wiki/The_Kingdom_of_Speech.

Wikipedia. 2024. "2000s United States Housing Bubble." Wikimedia Foundation. Last modified April 28, 2024. https://en.wikipedia.org/wiki/2000s_United_States_housing_bubble.

Wikipedia. 2024. "Bias." Wikimedia Foundation. Last modified April 6, 2024. http://en.wikipedia.org/wiki/Bias.

Wikipedia. 2024. "Dot-com Bubble." Wikimedia Foundation. Last modified May 3, 2024. http://en.wikipedia.org/wiki/Dot-com_bubble.

Wikipedia. 2024. "Myth of the Flat Earth." Wikimedia Foundation. Last modified April 29, 2024. https://en.wikipedia.org/wiki/Myth_of_the_flat_Earth.

Wikipedia. 2024. "Parthenon." Wikimedia Foundation. Last modified April 25, 2024. http://en.wikipedia.org/wiki/Parthenon.

Wikipedia. 2024. "Robert Hanssen." Wikimedia Foundation. Last modified April 26, 2024. http://en.wikipedia.org/wiki/Robert_Hanssen.

Wikipedia. 2024. "The Dress." Wikimedia Foundation. Last modified March 9, 2024. https://en.wikipedia.org/wiki/The_dress#Scientific_explanations.

Wikipedia. 2024. "The Truman Show." Wikimedia Foundation. Last modified May 1, 2024. https://en.wikipedia.org/wiki/The_Truman_Show.

Anglican Church in North America. *The Book of Common Prayer*. Huntington Beach, CA: Anglican Liturgy Press, 2019.

Ayman, Shahenda. "Do Women see More Colors than Men?" *SCIplanet* (November 23, 2017). Accessed December 29, 2021. https://www.bibalex.org/SCIplanet/en/Article/Details.aspx?id=10304.

Ball, Philip. "Smallest Genome Clocks in at 182 Genes." *Nature* (October 12, 2006). https://doi.org/10.1038/news061009-10. Accessed December 3, 2022.

Barry, J. D., and L. Wentz, eds. *The Lexham Bible Dictionary*. Bellingham, WA: Lexham Press, 2012.

Beckwith, Francis J., and Gregory Koukl. *Relativism: Feet Firmly Planted in Mid-Air.* Grand Rapids: Baker Books, 1998.

Behe, Michael J. *Darwin's Black Box: The Biochemical Challenge to Evolution.* New York: The Free Press, 1996.

Cabral, Carrie "Luke as a Historian: Is The Gospel Historically Correct?" *Shortform* (August 30, 2020). Accessed December 17, 2022. https://www.shortform.com/blog/luke-as-a-historian/.

Candy, Jim, Brad M. Griffin, and Kara Powell. *Can I Ask That?: 8 Hard Questions About God & Faith.* Pasadena, CA: Fuller Youth Institute, 2014.

Carlson, Richard F., ed. *Science and Christianity: Four Views.* Downers Grove, IL: InterVarsity Press, 2000.

Craig, William Lane. "God and the Beginning of Time." Reasonable Faith. Accessed May 4, 2019. https://www.reasonablefaith.org/writings/scholarly-writings/divine-eternity/god-and-the-beginning-of-time/.

———. *In Quest of the Historical Adam: A Biblical and Scientific Exploration.* Grand Rapids: Eerdmans, 2021.

———. *On Guard: Defending Your Faith with Reason and Precision.* 3rd ed. Colorado Springs, CO: David C. Cook, 2010.

Crossway Bibles. *The ESV Study Bible.* Wheaton, IL: Crossway Bibles, 2008.

Darwin, Charles. *The Descent of Man, and Selection in Relation to Sex: The Concise Edition.* London: Penguin Books Ltd., 2007.

———. (1859) 2004. *The Origin of Species.* New York: Barnes & Noble.

Davidson, Richard M. "In the Beginning: How to Interpret Genesis 1." *College and University Dialogue.* Accessed October 16, 2014. http://christintheclassroom.org/vol_26A/26a-cc_433-442.pdf.

Dembski, William A., and Michael Ruse, eds. (2004) 2007. *Debating Design: From Darwin to DNA.* New York: Cambridge University Press.

Dembski, William A., and Jonathan Wells. *The Design of Life: Discovering Signs of Intelligence in Biological Systems.* Dallas: The Foundation for Thought and Ethics, 2008.

Duignan, Brian. "Postmodernism." *Encyclopædia Britannica.* Accessed March 19, 2023. https://www.britannica.com/topic/postmodernism-philosophy.

Eberhard, David M., Gary F. Simons, and Charles D. Fennig (eds.). 2024. "How Many Languages in the World Are Unwritten?" *Ethnologue: Languages of the World.* Twenty-seventh edition. Dallas, Texas: SIL International. Accessed December 27, 2018. https://www.ethnologue.com/enterprise-faq/how-many-languages-world-are-unwritten-0.

Feldman, Richard. *Epistemology.* Upper Saddle River, NJ: Prentice Hall, 2003.

Gandhi, Maneka. "When Animals Shed Tears in Suffering." *Ocean Sentry* (March 7, 2009). Accessed March 26, 2020. https://www.oceansentry.org/when-animals-shed-tears-in-suffering/.

Gates, Bill. *The Road Ahead,* rev. ed. New York: Penguin Books, 1996.

Gertz, Bill. "Brian Kelley, Veteran Counterspy, Dies at 68." *The Washington Times* (Washington, DC), September 20, 2011. https://www.washingtontimes.com/news/2011/sep/20/brian-kelley-veteran-counterspy-dies-at-68/.

Gonzalez, Guillermo, and Jay W. Richards. *The Privileged Planet: How Our Place in the Cosmos Is Designed for Discovery.* Washington, DC: Regnery Publishing, Inc., 2004.

Gould, Stephen Jay. *Rocks of Ages: Science and Religion in the Fullness of Life.* New York: Random House Publishing, 1999.

Gregg, Steve. *Empire of the Risen Son: A Treatise on the Kingdom of God (Two Books in One Volume).* Maitland, FL: Xulon Press, 2021.

Hart-Davis, Adam. *Schrödinger's Cat: Fifty Experiments That Revolutionized Physics.* London: Elwin Street Productions Limited, 2015.

Heisenberg, Werner. *Physics and Philosophy: The Revolution in Modern Science.* London: Penguin Books, 1958.

Hendry, Lisa. "Why are birds the only surviving dinosaurs?" *The Natural History Museum.* Accessed June 21, 2022. https://www.nhm.ac.uk/discover/why-are-birds-the-only-surviving-dinosaurs.html#:~:text=Birds%20evolved%20from%20a%20group,about%20150%20million%20years%20old.

Hodge, Bodie, and Georgia Purdom. "Chapter 4 What Are 'Kinds' in Genesis?" *Answers in Genesis* (April 16, 2013). Accessed May 16, 2023. https://answersingenesis.org/creation-science/baraminology/what-are-kinds-in-genesis/.

Jones, Roger S. *Physics for the Rest of Us: Ten Basic Ideas of Twentieth-Century Physics That Everyone Should Know ... and How They Have Shaped Our Culture and Consciousness.* Chicago: Contemporary Books, 1992.

Kimball, John W. "Base Pairing." Kimball's Biology Pages. May 24, 2006. http://users.rcn.com/jkimball.ma.ultranet/BiologyPages/B/BasePairing.html.

Lewis, C. S. *A Grief Observed.* New York: HarperCollins, 1994.

———. *Mere Christianity.* San Francisco: HarperCollins, 1952.

Lightfoot, Neil R. *How We Got the Bible.* 3rd ed. Grand Rapids: Baker, 2004.

Linder, Doug. "The Trial of Jesus: An Account" (2002). Accessed July 10, 2022. http://law2.umkc.edu/faculty/projects/ftrials/jesus/jesusaccount.html#:~

:text=The%20gospels%20report%20that%20Jesus,the%20morning%20bef ore%20the%20Sanhedrin.

Litchfield, W. Reid. "The Search for the Physical Cause of Jesus Christ's Death." *Brigham Young University Studies* 37, no. 4 (1997): 93–109. Accessed February 6, 2023. https://www.jstor.org/stable/43044149.

McDowell, Josh D. *The New Evidence That Demands a Verdict.* Nashville: Thomas Nelson Publishers, 1999.

Merriam-Webster Dictionary. Merriam-Webster, Incorporated, Accessed July 4, 2023. https://www.merriam-webster.com.

Metaxas, Eric. "Is Archaeology Proving the Bible? | Opinion." *Newsweek* (October 4, 2021). Accessed December 17, 2022. https://www.newsweek.com/archaeology-proving-bible-opinion-1634339.

Meyer, Stephen C. *Darwin's Doubt: The Explosive Origin of Animal Life and the Case for Intelligent Design.* New York: HarperCollins, 2013.

———. *Signature in the Cell: DNA and the Evidence for Intelligent Design.* New York: HarperCollins, 2009.

Miller, Kenneth R. (1999) 2007. *Finding Darwin's God: A Scientist's Search for Common Ground Between God and Evolution.* New York: HarperCollins.

Montgomery, Stephen. "Life's Origins." *Charles Darwin & Evolution: 1809-2009.* Cambridge: Christ's College, 2009. Accessed December 12, 2013. https://darwin200.christs.cam.ac.uk/lifes-orgins.

Myers, Sheryl. "On Nature Column: Cells Function Like Miniature Cities." *The Herald Bulletin* (February 25, 2023). Accessed May 24, 2023. https://www.heraldbulletin.com/opinion/columns/on-nature-column-cells-function-like-miniature-cities/article_44855b6a-b391-11ed-99d5-cb5cee5b1193.html.

Oxford English Dictionary. Oxford University Press, Accessed June 30, 2020. https://public.oed.com.

Pascal, Blaise, 1623-1662. *Pascal's Pensées.* New York: E.P. Dutton, 1958.

Peretó, Juli, and Jesús Català. "Darwinism and the Origin of Life." *Evolution: Education and Outreach* (August 29, 2012). Accessed June 21, 2022. https://evolution-outreach.biomedcentral.com/articles/10.1007/s12052-012-0442-x.

Rana, Fazale, and Hugh Ross. *Who was Adam: A Creation Model Approach to the Origin of Man.* Colorado Springs, CO: NavPress, 2005.

Ross, Hugh. "Anthropic Principle vs Prebiotic Principle." *Reasons to Believe* (December 13, 2010). Accessed October 22, 2013. http://www.reasons.org/articles/anthropic-principle-vs-prebiotic-principle.

⸺⸺⸺. "Anthropic Principle: A Precise Plan for Humanity." *Reasons to Believe* (January 1, 2002). Accessed October 22, 2013. http://www.reasons.org/articles/anthropic-principle-a-precise-plan-for-humanity.

⸺⸺⸺. *The Fingerprint of God.* Pasadena, CA: Reasons to Believe, 1989.

Sanders, N.K. "The Epic of Gilgamesh." *Assyrian International News Agency.* Accessed October 24, 2014. http://www.aina.org/books/eog/eog.htm.

Slick, Matt. "Does the Genesis Creation Account Come From the Babylonian Enuma Elish?" *Christian Apologetics and Research Ministry (CARM)* (October 16, 2010). Accessed February 3, 2023. http://carm.org/genesis-creation-enuma-elish.

Sproul, R. C. *Reason to Believe: A Response to Common Objections to Christianity.* Grand Rapids: Zondervan, 1982.

Squires, Julie. "What Monkeys Can Teach Us: Letting Go." *Today's Veterinary Nurse* (March 1, 2016). Accessed January 16, 2023. https://todaysveterinarynurse.com/personal-wellbeing/what-monkeys-can-teach-us-letting-go/.

Stewart, Don. "What is textual criticism? Why is the textual criticism of the Bible necessary?" *Blue Letter Bible.* Accessed October 4, 2023. https://www.blueletterbible.org/Comm/stewart_don/faq/words-bible/question2-what-is-textual-criticism.cfm.

Strauss, Bob. "Pakicetus Facts and Figures." *ThoughtCo* (August 27, 2020). Accessed July 10, 2013. https://www.thoughtco.com/pakicetus-pakistan-whale-1093256.

Strobel, Lee. *The Case for Faith: A Journalist Investigates the Toughest Objections to Christianity.* Grand Rapids: Zondervan, 2000.

Taylor, Matt, and Rachel Taylor. "Is relativism and postmodernism the same?" *Seeking Our God* (August 18, 2014). Accessed March 19, 2023. https://seekingourgod.wordpress.com/2014/08/18/is-relativism-and-postmodernism-the-same/.

Understanding Evolution. University of California Museum of Paleontology. http://evolution.berkeley.edu/.

Wallace, J. Warner. *Cold-Case Christianity: A Homicide Detective Investigates the Claims of the Gospels.* Colorado Springs, CO: David C. Cook, 2013.

Wasserstein, Ronald L. "A Statistician's View: What Are Your Chances of Winning the Powerball Lottery?" *Huffington Post Science* (May 16, 2013). Accessed October 22, 2013. http://www.huffingtonpost.com/ronald-l-wasserstein/chances-of-winning-powerball-lottery_b_3288129.html.

Winters, Mike. "Here Are the Odds You'll Win the $439 Million Powerball Jackpot." *CNBC make it* (January 14, 2023). Accessed May 23, 2023. https://www.cnbc.com/2023/01/14/powerball-odds-of-winning-jackpot.html.

Wolper, David L. "Genesis and Science: More Aligned than You Think?" *Huff Post Religion* (May 15, 2010). Accessed January 7, 2015. http://www.huffingtonpost.com/david-l-wolper/genesis-and-science_b_500201.html.

End Notes

[1] Consider how, in just a few years, beliefs about marriage, human sexuality, and gender identity have become normalized in Western culture to the degree that it is no longer acceptable to question certain of those beliefs.

[2] Brian Duignan, "Postmodernism," *Encyclopædia Britannica*, accessed March 19, 2023, https://www.britannica.com/topic/postmodernism-philosophy.

[3] Matt Taylor and Rachel Taylor, "Is Relativism and Postmodernism the Same?," web log, *Seeking Our God* (blog), August 8, 2014, https://seekingourgod.wordpress.com/2014/08/18/is-relativism-and-postmodernism-the-same/.

[4] Ibid.

[5] *Merriam-Webster*, "Truth," accessed January 6, 2023, https://www.merriam-webster.com/dictionary/truth.

[6] *Merriam-Webster*, "Reality," accessed July 20, 2022, https://www.merriam-webster.com/dictionary/reality.

[7] Shahenda Ayman, "Do Women See More Colors than Men?," SCIplanet, November 23, 2017, http://www.bibalex.org/SCIplanet/en/Article/Details.aspx?id=10304.

[8] The ancient Parthenon was constructed between 447 and 431 BC, more than 2,400 years ago. When it was built, the columns of the Parthenon were intentionally angled in such a way as to create the illusion of being perfectly vertical. It is thought by some people to be a reverse optical illusion, combating the tendency of our minds to interpret a series of vertical columns as curved! Clearly, we have known for a long time the difference between the real and the illusory.
See Wikipedia, "Parthenon," 2024, http://en.wikipedia.org/wiki/Parthenon.

[9] Wikipedia, "The Dress," February 27, 2015, https://en.wikipedia.org/wiki/The_dress#Scientific_explanations.

[10] As bizarre as it seems, Truman was raised by people playing his family, who were in reality characters on the popular Truman Show.

[11] *Schrödinger's Cat* by Adam Hart-Davis provides a fascinating overview of the history behind our modern understanding of physics, depicting its growth as successive scientists built on the theories and discovery of earlier or contemporary scientists.

[12] Stephen Jay Gould, *Rocks of Ages: Science and Religion in the Fullness of Life* (New York: Random House Publishing, 1999), 111ff.

[13] Wikipedia, "Myth of the Flat Earth," January 3, 2023, https://en.wikipedia.org/wiki/Myth_of_the_flat_Earth.
John Draper and Andrew White popularized the myth to disparage Christians, in particular, who would not accept the relatively new evolutionary view of the development of life.

[14] *Merriam-Webster*, "Nature," accessed July 4, 2023, https://www.merriam-webster.com/dictionary/nature.

[15] J. Warner Wallace, *Cold-Case Christianity: A Homicide Detective Investigates the Claims of the Gospels* (Colorado Springs, CO: David C. Cook, 2013), 74-77.

[16] Even when people ascribed astronomical events (such as eclipses) to the actions of gods or perhaps magical forces, they were attempting to provide some set of reasons for the way the world worked. To our modern minds, those explanations come across as irrational, but that is because we have had thousands of years of investigation and thought to correct misconceptions. The people who were the first to propose reasons for such events and occurrences were thinking rationally within the framework of the knowledge they had and worldviews to which they adhered.

[17] It turns out that water molecules spread apart in the process of freezing, unlike most liquids in which the molecules slow down and become more tightly knit together. Don't we all slow down and bundle up when it gets really cold outside? Molecules do the same most of the time, but not with water. And so, ice cubes float because solid water (ice) is less compact or dense than liquid water. Now, you might next ask why *that* is so; that is the nature of our curious minds, always seeking to understand why the world is the way it is. And the answer to that question (about water) would lead us into a study of the hydrogen bonding between water molecules, which would then lead to a whole series of questions about molecules and the way they work.

[18] James Cameron, *True Lies* (United States: Twentieth Century Fox, 1994).

[19] "Reasonable Doubt," 'Lectric Law Library Lexicon, accessed June 2, 2022, https://www.lectlaw.com/def2/q016.htm.

[20] Brian Kelley passed away in September 2011.
Bill Gertz, "Brian Kelley, Veteran Counterspy, Dies at 68," *The Washington Times*, September 20, 2011, https://www.washingtontimes.com/news/2011/sep/20/brian-kelley-veteran-counterspy-dies-at-68/.

[21] Wikipedia, "Robert Hanssen," accessed June 2, 2022, http://en.wikipedia.org/wiki/Robert_Hanssen.

[22] Robert Hanssen died in prison on June 5, 2023.

[23] "Ice man" is a colloquialism referring to someone who is able to act calmly, without fear under extreme pressure or in extreme circumstances.

[24] Wikipedia, "Bias," accessed June 2, 2022, http://en.wikipedia.org/wiki/Bias.

[25] Julie Squires, "What Monkeys Can Teach Us: Letting Go," *Today's Veterinary Nurse*, March 1, 2016, https://todaysveterinarynurse.com/personal-wellbeing/what-monkeys-can-teach-us-letting-go/.

[26] Wikipedia, "Dot-com Bubble," accessed June 2, 2022, http://en.wikipedia.org/wiki/Dot-com_bubble.

[27] A similar thing happened with the recent housing bubble in the United States. Apart from the actions (or inactions) by politicians and banks that made it possible, the fact is that many people assumed that housing prices would continue to rise "forever," or at least long enough for them to cash in. Many people took out mortgages they could barely afford, counting on that growth and expecting to be able to sell their houses for much more than they paid for them or to be able to refinance their houses with the equity gained from rising values. But when the bubble burst and housing prices crashed, people who had lost their jobs now lost their homes as well. They couldn't afford the house payments, nor could they sell their houses for what they paid, and the banks foreclosed on large numbers of homeowners. People failed or refused to recognize that the housing market growth would one day come to an end, that the assumption of

unlimited growth was just that—an unfounded assumption. Consequently, they did not guard against that uncertainty through responsible borrowing and lending.

[28] The author asserts this as fact, having heard a 1953 recording of doctors advertising cigarettes as good for one's health.

[29] Needing a pronoun to refer to this "someone" in order to avoid awkward wording, I have chosen to use the third person masculine.

[30] Zulu, *Double Beaver Dam*, photograph, *FreeImages.Com*, accessed April 14, 2023, https://www.freeimages.com/photo/beaver-dam-1-1493167.

[31] William Lane Craig, *On Guard: Defending Your Faith with Reason and Precision*, 3rd ed. (Colorado Springs, CO: David C. Cook, 2010).
See 53-54 for Craig's formal presentation of the argument. Leibniz knew nothing of the elemental makeup of the universe (electrons, protons, neutrons, and so forth), whereas they are now integral to Craig's version of the argument.

[32] Ibid., 53.

[33] Ibid., 56 (italics original).

[34] Ibid., 60-63.

[35] There are scientists who propose the Multiverse Theory as a way of getting around this problem as well as the issues raised by the fine-tuning of the universe's properties, the Anthropic Principle that we will discuss shortly. The theory is that an uncountable number of other universes exist, and more are constantly being produced, each with structures and properties that are distinct from ours. We just happen to live in the one that has the properties that are perfect for life. It isn't surprising that out of a potentially infinite number of universes, one just happens to have the very attributes that our universe has—there is no need for a god to create our special universe.
See Craig, *On Guard,* 117-120, for a more detailed explanation of the theory and the flaws it has as a legitimate explanation for the existence of our universe.

[36] Craig, *On Guard,* 55-56.

[37] Ibid., 56.

[38] Ibid., 55.

[39] Ibid., 58-59.

[40] Ibid., 63.

[41] As used here, "gods" refers to imagined beings, often having superhuman or magical powers, whereas "God" refers to the kind of supernatural being postulated by Leibniz and Craig.

[42] Ibid., 87-88.

[43] Ibid., 90.
Craig presents additional philosophical and scientific arguments for the beginning of the universe; see 78-98.

[44] Ibid., 74.
The KCA is a medieval argument for God as the causal agent of the universe, whose main proponent was Muslim theologian Al-Ghazali.

[45] Ibid., 75.
Craig provides three reasons to accept the first premise as true (75-78).

[46] Ibid., 78-98.

[47] Ibid., 59.

[48] Ibid., 90.

[49] Ibid., 90-91.

I am using the term "self-existing" here and elsewhere as shorthand for something (the universe or God) that exists necessarily, without need of something or someone to bring it into existence.

[50] Ibid., 91-92.

[51] Hugh Ross, "Anthropic Principle: A Precise Plan for Humanity," Reasons to Believe, January 1, 2002, http://www.reasons.org/articles/anthropic-principle-a-precise-plan-for-humanity.

[52] Hugh Ross, "Anthropic Principle vs Prebiotic Principle," Reasons to Believe, December 13, 2010, http://www.reasons.org/articles/anthropic-principle-vs-prebiotic-principle.

[53] Ibid.

I combined the probabilities provided by Dr. Ross to arrive at the given number (accessed October 22, 2013).

[54] The probability of winning the Powerball jackpot is a little better than one-in-300 million.

Mike Winters, "Here Are the Odds You'll Win the $439 Million Powerball Jackpot," *CNBC make it*, January 14 2023, https://www.cnbc.com/2023/01/14/powerball-odds-of-winning-jackpot.html.

[55] Guillermo Gonzalez and Jay W. Richards, *The Privileged Planet: How Our Place in the Cosmos is Designed for Discovery* (Washington, DC: Regnery Publishing, Inc., 2004), Kindle location 5154.

[56] All boxed definitions of terms may be found in:

Learn.Genetics, University of Utah, accessed December 21, 2023.

http://learn.genetics.utah.edu

or

Stephen C. Meyer, *Darwin's Doubt: The Explosive Origin of Animal Life and the Case for Intelligent Design* (New York: HarperCollins, 2013), as follows:

- Mutation ("What is Mutation?" in Learn.Genetics)
- Natural Selection (*Darwin's Doubt,* 5)
- Intelligent Agent (*Darwin's Doubt,* 362)
- Common Descent (*Darwin's Doubt,* 4)
- Undirected (*Darwin's Doubt,* 410)
- Random (*Darwin's Doubt,* 10)

[57] "What is Mutation?," Learn.Genetics, accessed May 12, 2023, https://learn.genetics.utah.edu/content/basics/mutation#:~:text=Mutation%20creates%20slightly%20different%20versions,behavior%2C%20and%20susceptibility%20to%20disease.

Mutations can occur any time a cell divides, but we are interested only in mutations that are passed from one generation to the next.

[58] Charles Darwin, *The Origin of Species* (1859; repr., New York: Barnes & Noble, 2004), 60.

According to the copyright page, Darwin removed "On" from the title beginning with the second edition. The first edition, however, was used to prepare this version by Barnes & Noble.

[59] Ibid., 60-61, 111.

Darwin initially called this process the "struggle for existence" or "struggle for life." He will later refer to this natural process as "survival of the fittest."
See Charles Darwin, *The Descent of Man, and Selection in Relation to Sex: The Concise Edition* (London: Penguin Books Ltd., 2007), 204-205.

[60] "What is Mutation?," Learn.Genetics, accessed May 12, 2023, https://learn.genetics.utah.edu/content/basics/mutation.

[61] Bodie Hodge and Dr. Georgia Purdom, "Chapter 4: What Are 'Kinds' in Genesis?," Answers in Genesis, April 16, 2013, https://answersingenesis.org/creation-science/baraminology/what-are-kinds-in-genesis/.
While "kind" is not a term used by biologists, I will use "kind" and "family" interchangeably to refer generically to the highest level of distinction among biological organisms that is useful for discussing the merits of evolution.

[62] I am using the term "Darwinism" or "Darwinian evolution" in a general sense, not limiting it to Darwin's time. That is, "Neo-Darwinism" is included in my usage, the distinction between the terms not being important for this discussion. Neo-Darwinism expresses Darwinian evolution in terms of our 20th to 21st century knowledge of genetics, random genetic change (mutation) being the fuel that feeds Darwin's engine of natural selection. Accordingly, the essential principles proposed by Darwin remain unchanged, so that my treatment of Darwinian evolution is inclusive of the most recent understandings.

[63] The word "organism" is used throughout this section as an all-inclusive reference to any and all kinds of living things.

[64] "Intelligent agent" is a general term for any agent (animal, person, or other being) with the capacity to envision a desired outcome and purposely act to achieve that result.

[65] Regardless of your view of the earth's age, the argument for a creator's involvement in the development of life remains largely the same.

[66] Lisa Hendry, "Why Are Birds the Only Surviving Dinosaurs?," The Natural History Museum, accessed June 21, 2022, https://www.nhm.ac.uk/discover/why-are-birds-the-only-surviving-dinosaurs.html.

[67] Darwin, *The Origin of Species*, 380.

[68] *Merriam-Webster*, "Undirected," accessed July 26, 2023, https://www.merriam-webster.com/dictionary/undirected.

[69] *Merriam-Webster*, "Random," accessed July 26, 2023, https://www.merriam-webster.com/dictionary/random.

[70] For example, see "Transitional Features," Understanding Evolution, University of California Museum of Paleontology, accessed April 12, 2024, https://evolution.berkeley.edu/lines-of-evidence/transitional-features/, the details of which I address in my discussion of the Pakicetus and Eohippus. In the article, we read such things as, "We *know* that pakicetids were closely related to whales and dolphins based on a number of unique specializations of the ear," and "The ancestors of whales *probably* looked something like *Pakicetus*." These are not statements of scientific knowledge; rather, they're hypotheses that need to be proven.

[71] "God-of-the-Gaps" refers to explanations of phenomena that use God as the explanation for what science has yet to understand and explain by reference to natural cause and effect.

[72] William A. Dembski and Jonathan Wells, *The Design of Life: Discovering Signs of Intelligence in Biological Systems* (Dallas: The Foundation for Thought and Ethics, 2008), 60.

[73] Darwin, *The Origin of Species,* 243-250.

[74] Dembski and Wells, 62, 72-73.

[75] Ibid., 62-64.

[76] Ibid., 64.

[77] Ibid., 42.

[78] Hendry, https://www.nhm.ac.uk/discover/why-are-birds-the-only-surviving-dinosaurs.html.

[79] Understanding Evolution, University of California Museum of Paleontology, accessed July 10, 2013, https://evolution.berkeley.edu.

[80] Bob Strauss, "Pakicetus Facts and Figures," *ThoughtCo,* August 27, 2020, https://www.thoughtco.com/pakicetus-pakistan-whale-1093256.

[81] "Transitional Features," Understanding Evolution, University of California Museum of Paleontology, June 2020, http://evolution.berkeley.edu/evosite/lines/IAtransitional.shtml.

[82] Ibid.

[83] Ibid.

[84] Ibid.

[85] Ibid.

[86] Ibid.

[87] "Phylum," BiologyOnline, accessed May 18, 2023, https://www.biologyonline.com/dictionary/phylum.

[88] Dembski and Wells, 63.

[89] Ibid., 63-64.

Merriam-Webster, "Morphology," accessed July 26, 2023, https://www.merriam-webster.com/dictionary/morphology.

[90] Dembski and Wells, 63-64.

[91] Darwin, *The Origin of Species,* 243-246.

[92] William A. Dembski and Michael Ruse, eds., *Debating Design: From Darwin to DNA* (2004; repr., New York: Cambridge University Press, 2007), 24-25.

[93] Kenneth R. Miller, *Finding Darwin's God: A Scientist's Search for Common Ground Between God and Evolution* (1999; repr., New York: HarperCollins, 2007), 82-87.

[94] Dembski and Wells, 75.

[95] Ibid., 38-39.

[96] Ibid., 38, 45, 51.

[97] Darwin, *The Origin of Species,* 44-45, 52.

[98] Ibid., 316-317.

[99] Ibid., 249.

[100] "DNA" is the molecule that carries the genetic code for all living things. See Appendix B: A Brief Review of Genetics for a simplified explanation of DNA.

[101] Dembski and Wells, 32-33, 38.

[102] Bill Gates, *The Road Ahead*, rev. ed. (New York: Penguin Books, 1996), 228.

103 Sheryl Myers, "On Nature Column: Cells Function Like Miniature Cities," *The Herald Bulletin*, February 25, 2023, https://www.heraldbulletin.com/opinion/columns/on-nature-column-cells-function-like-miniature-cities/article_44855b6a-b391-11ed-99d5-cb5cee5b1193.html.

104 Philip Ball, "Smallest Genome Clocks in at 182 Genes," *nature*, October 12, 2006, https://www.nature.com/news/2006/061009/full/news061009-10.html.

105 "Size Matters: A Whole Genome Is 6.4B Letters," Veritas, July 28, 2017, https://www.veritasgenetics.com/our-thinking/whole-story/.

106 The problem for evolution is actually much bigger; if evolution is true, then all life (including us) evolved from a first *single-celled* organism. Further, evolutionists must assume the "creation" by nature of that first single-celled organism (called "abiogenesis"), but they have no verifiable hypothesis for how such a thing could happen.

107 For instance, the bacterium reproduces asexually, whereas human reproduction requires a male and a female counterpart. It is not clear how such a transformation would be possible while maintaining and improving survivability.

108 Dembski and Wells, 44.

109 Dembski and Ruse, 331.

110 Ibid., 331.

111 Michael J. Behe, *Darwin's Black Box: The Biochemical Challenge to Evolution* (New York: The Free Press, 1996), 39-45.

112 Stephen C. Meyer, *Signature in the Cell: DNA and the Evidence for Intelligent Design* (New York: HarperCollins, 2009), 105-110.

113 Behe, 39.

114 Ibid., 42.

115 Meyer, *Signature in the Cell*, 105-108.

116 Ibid., 108. Used given probability calculation ($p = (1/4)^n$) for a nucleotide of 500 pairs [9.33×10^{-302}].

117 The probability of winning the Powerball jackpot is a little better than one-in-300 million.
Mike Winters, https://www.cnbc.com/2023/01/14/powerball-odds-of-winning-jackpot.html.

118 Meyer, *Signature in the Cell*, 107-109.

119 Ibid., 290-295.

120 *Merriam-Webster*, "Abiogenesis," accessed July 26, 2023, https://www.merriam-webster.com/dictionary/abiogenesis.

121 Myers, "On Nature Column: Cells Function Like Miniature Cities."

122 Masculine pronoun used to avoid cumbersome language.

123 Werner Heisenberg, *Physics and Philosophy: The Revolution in Modern Science* (London: Penguin Books, 1958), 52.

124 Maneka Gandhi, "When Animals Shed Tears in Suffering," *Ocean Sentry*, March 7, 2009, https://www.oceansentry.org/when-animals-shed-tears-in-suffering/.

125 "World Languages," DayTranslations, accessed July 18, 2018, https://www.daytranslations.com/world-languages.

[126] "How Many Languages in the World Are Unwritten?," *Ethnologue: Languages of the World*, accessed December 27, 2018, https://www.ethnologue.com/enterprise-faq/how-many-languages-world-are-unwritten-0.

[127] Another difficult (or insurmountable) problem for evolution. Tom Wolfe's *The Kingdom of Speech* has an interesting take on this from someone who would otherwise disagree with my conclusions in this book. "Wolfe argues that speech, not evolution, sets humans apart from animals and is responsible for all of humanity's complex achievements."
Wikipedia, "The Kingdom of Speech," accessed February 2, 2023, https://en.wikipedia.org/wiki/The_Kingdom_of_Speech.

[128] *Oxford English Dictionary*, "Updates to the OED," June 2020, https://public.oed.com/updates/.

[129] *Oxford English Dictionary*, "History of the OED," accessed June 30, 2020, https://public.oed.com/history/.

[130] William Lane Craig, *In Quest of the Historical Adam: A Biblical and Scientific Exploration* (Grand Rapids: Eerdmans, 2021), 258.
Craig lists the characteristics identified by anthropologists Sally McBrearty and Alison Brooks that uniquely identify modern human behavior.

[131] Called the "Anthropic Principle," scientists have discovered more than 800 fundamental properties of the universe that were so finely tuned when the universe began that even a minor change to just one of those properties would have made this planet unfit for human habitation. The Anthropic Principle is just the type of circumstantial evidence we would expect to find if God purposely created the universe with humans (and animals and vegetation) in mind.
Hugh Ross, "Anthropic Principle vs Prebiotic Principle."

[132] "Do Dogs Dream?" *Purina*, accessed April 11, 2024, https://www.purina.co.uk/articles/dogs/behaviour/common-questions/do-dogs-dream.

[133] I will refer to the creator of the world as "God," fully recognizing that the word "God" is a vague term that can have various meanings for people of different beliefs. Also, I will capitalize "Creator" in further usage when the word clearly points to God the Creator.

[134] "God-speech" emphasizes God's willful action in communicating with us, in contrast to our communication with Him.

[135] "The Changing Global Religious Landscape," April 5, 2017, Pew Research Center, http://www.pewforum.org/2017/04/05/the-changing-global-religious-landscape/.

[136] Most biblical writings are not nearly as long as our modern books. For instance, Genesis, the first and one of the longest biblical writings, contains approximately 38,000 English words or about 100 pages formatted as we do today. Other biblical writings are actually letters, not intended to be books at all. Nonetheless, it is common practice to refer to the individual biblical writings generically as "books."

[137] Neil R. Lightfoot, *How We Got the Bible*, 3rd edition (Grand Rapid: Baker, 2004), 23-24.

[138] Ibid., 24.

[139] While God's purpose in establishing a covenant is always stated, God's reasons for selecting this person (or group of people) but not that person (or group) for

accomplishing that purpose do not usually become evident until the unfolding of the events that follow.

[140] The inhabitants of the modern nation of Israel are called "Israelis." While many Israelis are descendants of the ancient Israelites (especially from the tribe of Judah), most of the descendants of the ancient twelve tribes of Israel are scattered among the nations of the world.

[141] "Scriptures" is a word from the Latin, meaning "writings."

[142] Some of the books of the Bible were written solely by one author while others were a compilation of prior writings, sometimes with additions by the compiler. For simplicity, however, I generically refer to all the books as written.

[143] *The Holy Bible: English Standard Version*, Genesis 1:1, meaning Genesis chapter 1, verse 1. The books of the Bible did not originally have the chapter or verse divisions that we have today; they were added much later to make it easier to reference specific portions of the Bible. All biblical references are from the English Standard Version (ESV), unless otherwise stated.

[144] "Notes for Gen. 1:1," *The NET Bible First Edition Notes* (Biblical Studies Press, 2006).

[145] This is consistent with the Kalām Cosmological Argument in Chapter 3, which concludes that the universe must have a cause.

[146] William Lane Craig, "God and the Beginning of Time," Reasonable Faith, accessed May 4, 2019, https://www.reasonablefaith.org/writings/scholarly-writings/divine-eternity/god-and-the-beginning-of-time/.
Also see: Richard M. Davidson, "In the Beginning: How to Interpret Genesis 1," *College and University Dialogue*, accessed October 16, 2014, http://christintheclassroom.org/vol_26A/26a-cc_433-442.pdf.

[147] Roger S. Jones, *Physics for the Rest of Us: Ten Basic Ideas of Twentieth-Century Physics That Everyone Should Know … and How They Have Shaped Our Culture and Consciousness* (Chicago: Contemporary Books, 1992), 76.
Einstein initially refused to accept the prediction of his own theory until the observations of Edwin Hubble (of the galactic redshift) confirmed the expansion of the universe. Einstein even added a fudge factor to his equations (the so-called "cosmological constant") to avoid the inference that the universe had a beginning, because *that* implied the existence of a being who brought the universe into existence, something Einstein was unwilling to accept at that point in his life.

[148] Matt Slick, "Does the Genesis Creation Account Come From the Babylonian Enuma Elish?," October 16, 2010, Christian Apologetics and Research Ministry (CARM), http://carm.org/genesis-creation-enuma-elish.

[149] For a description of the Roman gods and goddesses, see "The Gods and Goddesses of Ancient Rome." *National Geographic: Education*, accessed April 11, 2024, https://education.nationalgeographic.org/resource/gods-and-goddesses-ancient-rome/.

[150] Gen. 1:26, 28.

[151] Gen. 1:31.

[152] "The Fall" refers to the disobedience of the first humans and its consequences. "The Flood" refers to the Great Flood of Noah's days. We will look at both stories as we work through Genesis.

[153] N. K. Sanders, "The Epic of Gilgamesh," Assyrian International News Agency, accessed October 24, 2014, http://www.aina.org/books/eog/eog.htm.

This epic is not strictly a creation story, but it does have a few common themes and suffices to demonstrate the true character of myth, as the non-scholar typically understands that term.

154 The meaning of "day" in Genesis 1 is an ongoing topic of controversy, even among those who accept Genesis as a revelation from God. One of the main views is that the Genesis day is a literal 24-hour period (an evening and a morning), while the primary contrasting view is that each day refers metaphorically to the beginning of a geological age. For our purposes, the actual meaning of "day" is not as important as what the counting of each day signifies: Time began to be reckoned with the creation of the heavens and the earth.

155 See Chapter 4 of this book for a discussion of adaptation and the varieties that result.

156 The manner of revelation is not important. It could be directly from God to the author, or indirectly through one or more intermediaries. Moreover, it could be that God revealed the account to those who passed it along by word-of-mouth from generation to generation until someone finally wrote it down in the book of Genesis.

157 David L. Wolper, "Genesis And Science: More Aligned Than You Think?," *Huff Post Religion*, May 15, 2010, http://www.huffingtonpost.com/david-l-wolper/genesis-and-science_b_500201.html.

158 The Cambrian Explosion (see Chapter 4 of this book) is one such example, inexplicable according to evolutionary theory but perfectly compatible with the Genesis creation account.

159 Our interest in God-speech goes beyond God's act of creation; we want to know whether God speaks *to and with* the rational beings He created. In fact, the Bible records God's regular interaction with humanity: Of the 23,145 verses in the Old Testament (OT), God is identified as the speaker in 5,879 verses, about 25% of all OT verses. There are 7,957 verses in the New Testament (NT), and God the Father or Jesus the Son speak in 2,112 verses, more than 25% of all NT verses. The total verse counts are from: Wikipedia, "Chapters and Verses of the Bible." *Logos* searches were used to determine the number of verses in which God and/or Jesus spoke.

160 "YHWH" in the Hebrew, pronounced "Yahweh," is the name God gives for Himself when Moses asks what the people of Israel should call Him (Exod. 3:15).

161 Gen. 2:9.

162 Whether Adam and Eve would have been familiar with death at this point is a subject of controversy that depends on one's understanding of what it means for creation to be "good." Fossil fuels, for example, come from decayed remains of bacteria, plants, and animals. Consequently, it is possible that natural death from aging rather than from predation could be consistent with Genesis 1:30 and could even be a necessary good for the sustenance of life on Earth. If so, Adam and Eve could at least have had some concept of what it means to die.

163 While Genesis does not explicitly refer to a controlling entity, "the narrative itself implies [that there is one], given the serpent's ability to speak and the vile things he says" (*The ESV Study Bible*. Wheaton, IL: Crossway Bibles. Genesis 3:15). Revelation 12:9 and 20:2 identify "the ancient serpent" as "the devil and Satan" and imply that this serpent is the same one found in the Garden of Eden. The oldest direct reference to

Satan is in the book of Job, chapters 1 and 2, where we see that he is an angelic being and an adversary of human beings, which is what his name means.

[164] We are not told directly why Satan wanted to destroy humanity, but his actions were (and are) apparently driven by pride; he sought to make himself equal with God, wanting human beings to worship him rather than their Creator. This is based on a proposed theological understanding of Isa. 14:12-14 and Ezek. 28:12-18. J. D. Barry and L. Wentz, eds., *The Lexham Bible Dictionary* (Bellingham, WA: Lexham Press, 2012).

[165] Gen. 3:1.

[166] Gen. 3:4-5.

[167] Gen. 3:6.

[168] Creation is separate from God, so the evil that entered creation does not impugn God's goodness.

[169] It is not my intent to weigh in on the question of election in this book, that is, whether God predestines certain people to enter into a restored and saving relationship with Him. In the next chapter, I will merely present the Gospel, that all who place their faith in Jesus Christ—however that happens—will be saved.

[170] Gen. 3:7.

[171] Gen. 3:8-9.

[172] Gen. 3:11.

[173] This is the first instance in the Bible of human beings responding to God.

[174] Gen. 3:14-15.

[175] The Hebrew is in the singular.

[176] It is, perhaps, a clue to what Eve's offspring will suffer, that God removes the fig leaves with which Adam and Eve had clothed themselves and clothes them instead with "garments of skin" (Gen. 3:21). The garments provided by God required the death of an animal, suggesting that the sin of Adam and Eve could be covered only by the shedding of blood, the death of some animal. As we will see, the ultimate covering for all humanity's sin would require the death of one of Eve's descendants.

[177] God's promise in Genesis is clearly meant to be a foretelling of future events—what we would call a "prophecy." God is not constrained by, but rather lives apart from, our world of space and time. That being the case, it does seem to be consistent with God's eternal nature that He would know how future events in His creation would unfold. The Bible is filled with prophetic utterances of future events that come to pass according to what was prophesied.

[178] Gen. 2:24.

[179] Gen. 3:16.

[180] Gen. 3:19.

[181] Gen. 3:8.

[182] While not all Christians believe that children are born with a sin nature, tainted by the sin of Adam and Eve, all Christians acknowledge that no person lives long without disobeying God and becoming separated from Him.

[183] Genesis 6:6 reads, "The LORD regretted that he had made human beings on the earth, and his heart was deeply troubled." Did God think He had made a mistake? No, it's more likely that God regretted the way men and women were continuously doing

evil to one another; He was broken-hearted over the pain and suffering people were causing each other.

[184] Whether the Noahic Flood was global or something less extensive, my focus is on the fact that God did something about evil. It would be easy to get lost in disputes over the evidence for a global flood and be blinded to the extent of human evil and God's response to it.

[185] Steve Gregg, *Empire of the Risen Son: A Treatise on the Kingdom of God (Two Books in One Volume)* (Maitland, FL: Xulon Press, 2021), 71.

[186] Gen. 22:18. Abram means "exalted father." God will change Abram's name to "Abraham," meaning "father of a multitude," in anticipation of the birth of the promised son, Isaac, and the descendants who will come from him (Gen. 17:5). Abram's wife, Sarai, will also have her name changed by God, to "Sarah" (Gen. 17:15). Since both names mean "princess," this name change may be largely symbolic, indicating a change in status before God.

[187] Scripture referenced in this paragraph from: Gen. 6, 12, 17.

[188] Scripture referenced in this paragraph from: Gen. 28, 32, 49; 1 Chron. 16.

[189] Scripture referenced in this paragraph from: Exod. 3; Deut. 18.

[190] Mic. 5:5; italics added to emphasize that the One to come would not merely usher in peace (perhaps as a conquering leader) but would be the very source of the people's peace.

[191] Scripture referenced in this paragraph from: 1 Sam. 8, 24; 2 Sam. 7, 12; Ps. 2; Isa. 7; Mic. 5; Matt. 1.

[192] Scripture referenced in the following list from: Isa. 42, 53, 61.

[193] Scripture referenced in the following list from: Gen. 3; Jer. 31; Dan. 7, 9; Zech. 9.

[194] Josh D. McDowell, *The New Evidence That Demands a Verdict* (Nashville: Thomas Nelson Publishers, 1999), 119-120.

Few people today dispute the existence of a real person named Jesus who lived in first-century Israel, and that He is the person the Gospel authors wrote about.

See Appendix E: Trustworthiness of the New Testament for insights into the reliability of our modern New Testament texts.

[195] In the New Testament church, an apostle was someone who was *sent* out to spread the Gospel, the Good News about Jesus. The English word "apostle" is a transliteration of the Greek word ἀποστόλος, meaning "sent one."

[196] C. S. Lewis, *Mere Christianity* (San Francisco: HarperCollins, 1952), 52.

[197] Ibid., 52.

[198] 2 Cor. 5:19, 1 Pet. 2:22, 1 John 3:5.

[199] For several hundred years after Christ, many leaders in the Christian Church attempted explanations as to how such a thing was possible—all fraught with inherent contradictions; thus, acknowledging that Jesus's dual nature could not be understood solely by human reasoning, the Church simply affirmed it as the teaching of Scripture in the Chalcedonian Creed at the Council of Chalcedon in AD 451.

[200] Scripture referenced in this paragraph from: Matt. 1, 14; Mark 1, 3; Luke 2, 22; John 1, 3, 5, 8, 17; Mal. 4.

²⁰¹ In the context of this Scripture (Luke 1:32-33), "father" refers not to Jesus's biological ancestor but to His lineage by virtue of His parents (Luke 3:23-34, Matt. 1:1-16) in the tribe of Judah from which the Messiah was promised (Gen. 49:10).

²⁰² Scripture referenced in this paragraph from: Matt. 1; Luke 1, 2; John 1.

²⁰³ Scripture referenced in this paragraph from: Matt. 3, 4; Mark 1, 3; Luke 3, 4; John 1, 2. The disciples' understanding of who the Messiah was and what He would do continues to grow throughout Jesus's time with them, but they won't fully comprehend Jesus's teaching about Himself until after He is raised from the dead.

²⁰⁴ Matthew refers to the kingdom of God five times but refers to the kingdom of heaven 32 times. For our purposes, they both signifying the realm of God's reign. The other Gospels refer only to the kingdom of God.

²⁰⁵ Scripture referenced in this paragraph from: Matt. 4, 8, 9, 21; Mark 1, 2, 7, 10; Luke 3, 4, 6, 13; John 3, 9, 20. By my count, the Gospels record eight distinctive miracles that reveal Jesus's authority over the physical world, 14 separate healings of people with disabilities, five specific healings of people with various diseases, seven documented deliverances from demonic spirits, and three instances of Jesus raising people from the dead. In addition to these 37 unique examples of Jesus's authority over all creation, the Gospels record a number of times that Jesus "went throughout all the cities and villages, teaching in their synagogues and proclaiming the Gospel of the kingdom and healing every disease and every affliction" (Matt. 9:35).
See Appendix D: The Gospels' Description of Jesus, for a detailed list of Jesus's healings and miracles.

²⁰⁶ Scripture referenced in this paragraph from: Matt. 4, 7, 11, 12, 13, 15, 16, 23; Mark 1, 2, 3, 4, 11,12; Luke 4, 5, 6; John 3, 5, 7, 9, 11, 12.

²⁰⁷ Scripture referenced in this paragraph from: Matt. 5—7, 16, 21, 22; Mark 1, 7, 8, 9; Luke 3, 5, 9, 13; John 5, 7, 8, 14.

²⁰⁸ Scripture referenced in this paragraph from: Matt. 16, 17, 19, 20, 22, 26; Mark 1, 7, 8, 11, 14; Luke 4, 9, 13, 14, 22, 23; John 1, 4, 5, 6, 7, 8, 9, 10, 11, 12, 14, 17.

²⁰⁹ Scripture referenced in this paragraph from: Matt. 26; Mark 14; Luke 22; John 13, 18.

²¹⁰ The text actually refers to "another disciple." He is assumed to be the apostle John who is the presumed author of John's Gospel, "the disciple whom Jesus loved" (John 13:23, John 19:26, John 20:2, John 21:7, John 21:20).

²¹¹ Scripture referenced in this paragraph from: Matt. 26; Mark 14; John 13, 18.

²¹² According to Doug Linder, "The Trial of Jesus: An Account," 2002, http://law2.umkc.edu/faculty/projects/ftrials/jesus/jesusaccount.html, there is some discrepancy about when and where the trial(s) of Jesus occurred. For my purposes, it is sufficient to say that Jesus was tried and condemned.

²¹³ Scripture referenced in this paragraph from: Matt. 26, 27; Mark 11, 15; John 11.

²¹⁴ Scripture referenced in this paragraph from: Mark 15; John 19.

²¹⁵ According to the ESV Study Bible, "The curtain between the Holy Place and the Most Holy Place was an elaborately woven fabric of 72 twisted plaits of 24 threads each. It was 60 feet (18 m) high and 30 feet (9.1 m) wide." Consequently, the sudden tearing of the curtain from top to bottom could not have been accomplished by any human means of the time.

²¹⁶ Scripture referenced in this paragraph from: Matt. 27; Mark 15; Luke 23; John 19, 20. Whether we have the exact words of the centurion (Luke 23:47; Matt. 27:54; Mark

15:39), the more important point is that the man who had no doubt witnessed the death of many people, by crucifixion in particular, clearly had never seen anything like the way Jesus willingly died and the signs that accompanied His death.

[217] Psalm 34:20 prophesies that Jesus's bones will not be broken. Modern investigations into the effects of flogging and crucifixion support John's observations (John 19:34-35), although what John calls water is actually the clear pericardial fluid that would have pooled around Jesus's heart as a result of His scourging (Litchfield, 1997; Got Questions, 2023; Wilson, 1979).

[218] Scripture referenced in this paragraph from: Matt. 27; Mark 15; Luke 23, 24; John 19, 20.

[219] Scripture referenced in this paragraph from: Matt. 27:62-66.

[220] The Gospels differ in their descriptions of which women went to the tomb; John indicates that it was only Mary Magdalene (John 20:1) and Matthew has "the other Mary" with Mary Magdalene (Matt. 28:1). Mark identifies "the other Mary" as the mother of James and includes Salome as one of the women who went to the tomb (Mark 16:1). Luke does not tell us who went to the tomb (Luke 24:1), but names "Mary Magdalene and Joanna and Mary the mother of James and the other women with them" as those who told the disciples what they had seen (Luke 24:10).

[221] Scripture referenced in the following list from: Matt. 28; Mark 16; Luke 24; John 20.

[222] The New Testament does not yet exist. The Gospels and other New Testament books will be written over the course of the next 60 years.

[223] The apostle Paul will later testify that Jesus "appeared to [Peter], then to the twelve. Then He appeared to more than five hundred brothers at one time, most of whom are still alive …. Then He appeared to James, then to all the apostles. Last of all, as to one untimely born, He appeared also to me" (1 Cor. 15:5-8).

[224] Scripture referenced in this paragraph from: Luke 24; John 20.

[225] Scripture referenced in this paragraph from: Luke 24; John 20; Acts 1.

[226] Acts 2:1-4.

[227] Those who doubted were likely disciples other than the eleven who accompanied Jesus throughout His ministry.

[228] Scripture referenced in this paragraph from: Matt. 28; Luke 24; Acts 1.

[229] Scripture referenced in this paragraph from: Acts 1, 2.

[230] Acts 2:22-24.

[231] Scripture referenced in this paragraph from: Acts 2.

[232] Scripture referenced in this paragraph from: Acts 2, 9, 24. The twelve are now called "apostles" (meaning "sent ones"), being sent by Jesus to spread the Gospel to the nations. The first believers were fully Jewish, maintaining Jewish religious practices but expressing faith in Jesus as their Messiah.

[233] Scripture referenced in this paragraph from: Acts 3, 4.

[234] Scripture referenced in this paragraph from: Acts 5, 6, 7, 8, 9, 13. Acts 6:1-6 describes the appointing of those we now refer to as "deacons" (a transliteration of the Greek διακονος, meaning "servant").

[235] Scripture referenced in this paragraph from: Matt. 28; Mark 16; Rom. 8; Gal. 2; Phil. 3.

236 "The Global Religious Landscape," Pew Research Center, December 18, 2012, https://www.pewresearch.org/religion/2012/12/18/global-religious-landscape-exec/.

237 1 Cor. 15:17.

238 Jesus's resurrection is distinguished from other examples described in Scriptures (such as that of Lazarus, discussed earlier) in that Jesus—having lived a perfect life—was resurrected to eternal life. The others who experienced resurrection ultimately died once again but will be raised with all believers to eternal life on the last day.

239 McDowell, 193-194.

240 Ibid., 193.

241 Matt. 28:18-20; Mark 16:6-7; Luke 1:1-4; John 19:35, John 20:31, 1 John 5:13.

242 Luke 7:22.

243 Matt. 12:9-14; Mark 3:1-6, Mark 5:35-43; Luke 6:6-11, Luke 13:10-17, Luke 14:1-6; John 5:9-16, John 7:21-24, John 12:42-43. See Appendix D: The Gospels' Description of Jesus for a list of the healings, exorcisms, miracles, and resurrections performed by Jesus; these testify to the Divine anointing on Jesus's life and ministry.

244 John 19:31-34.

245 Matt. 27:62-66.

246 Acts 12:18-19 is an example of what happened to guards who failed. In Acts 16:25-30, we see that the Philippian jailer would rather kill himself than to suffer the judgment for failing to keep his prisoners.

247 Scriptures referenced in this paragraph from: Matt. 28; Mark 16; Luke 24; John 20.

248 Scriptures referenced in this paragraph from: Matt. 28; Mark 16; Luke 24; John 20.

249 Scriptures referenced in this paragraph from: Matt. 28; Mark 16; Luke 24; John 20; Acts 1.

250 Scriptures referenced in this paragraph from: Acts 2, 4, 12.

251 Scriptures referenced in this paragraph from: Acts 3, 4, 9, 14, 16, 20, 28; 1 Cor. 12; James 5.

252 Scriptures referenced in this paragraph from: Acts 2, 5, 11.

253 Scriptures referenced in this paragraph from: Acts 9; 2 Cor. 11; Gal. 1.

254 McDowell, 55.

255 Ibid., 55.

256 Ibid., 57.

257 Ibid., 58

258 C. S. Lewis, *A Grief Observed* (New York: HarperCollins, 1994), 22.

259 Craig, *On Guard*, 63.

260 Gen. 1:26-27.

261 Scriptures referenced in this paragraph from: Gen. 1; Deut. 4; Luke 11.

262 Isa. 53:4-6, 10-12; John 3:16-17; 1 Cor. 15:3-8; Eph. 2:13-19.

263 Ps. 14:1-3; Isa. 53:6, Isa. 59:1-8; Rom. 3:9-18, Rom. 3:23, Rom. 5:12-14.

264 Isa. 59:1-2; Rom. 3:19-20, Rom. 5:18; Eph. 2:11-12.

265 Gen. 3:15; 1 Cor. 15:24-28; Heb. 2:14-18; Rev. 12:7-11.

266 John 3:16-18.

267 Scriptures referenced in this paragraph from: Acts 1, 2; Rom. 8, 12; 1 Cor. 15; 2 Cor. 5; Gal. 5, 6; Eph. 6; Titus 2; Heb. 10.

268 John 1:3; John 1:14.

269 Darwin, *The Origin of Species*, 384.

[270] Stephen Montgomery, *Charles Darwin & Evolution: 1809-2009* (Cambridge: Christ's College, 2009), https://darwin200.christs.cam.ac.uk/lifes-orgins.

[271] Juli Peretó and Jesús Català, "Darwinism and the Origin of Life." *Evolution: Education and Outreach*, August 29, 2012, accessed June 21, 2022, https://evolution-outreach.biomedcentral.com/articles/10.1007/s12052-012-0442-x.

[272] Darwin, *The Origin of Species,* 228ff.

[273] Ibid., 378.

[274] Miller, 32.

[275] Darwin, *The Origin of Species,* 243-250.

[276] Dembski and Wells, 32, 38, 43.

[277] Ibid., 38-39, 45.

[278] Ibid., 104.

[279] Ibid., 102-104.

[280] Myers, "On Nature Column: Cells Function Like Miniature Cities."

[281] Ibid.

[282] The University of Utah's Learn.Genetics website is an easy-to-use and easy-to-follow introduction to the basics (http://learn.genetics.utah.edu).

[283] John W.Kimball, "Base Pairing," Kimball's Biology Pages, May 24, 2006, http://users.rcn.com/jkimball.ma.ultranet/BiologyPages/B/BasePairing.html.

[284] "The Science Behind the Human Genome Project," Human Genome Project Information, U.S. Department of Energy Office of Science, Office of Biological and Environmental Research, Human Genome Program, March 26, 2008, http://web.ornl.gov/sci/techresources/Human_Genome/project/info.shtml.

[285] Ibid.

[286] *File:DNA-Structure-and-Bases.Png*, 2010, photograph, *Wikimedia Commons* , 2010, http://commons.wikimedia.org/wiki/File:DNA-structure-and-bases.png.

[287] "Logos Bible Software" is a software application of Faithlife Corporation containing searchable digital versions of the Bible. A "Logos search" exploits this capability according to the syntax rules of the software.

[288] Eric Metaxas, "Is Archaeology Proving the Bible? | Opinion," *Newsweek*, October 4, 2021, https://www.newsweek.com/archaeology-proving-bible-opinion-1634339.

[289] Carrie Cabral, "Luke as a Historian: Is the Gospel Historically Correct?," Shortform, Aug 30, 2020, https://www.shortform.com/blog/luke-as-a-historian/.

[290] "55 Old Testament Prophecies about Jesus," Jesus Film Project: A CRU Ministry, November 17, 2021, https://www.jesusfilm.org/blog/old-testament-prophecies/.

[291] This appendix is neither a scholarly study of the Scriptures to classify every pertinent Gospel passage nor a rigorous approach in determining whether a claim applies to Jesus's human or His Divine nature.

[292] Gregg, 58.

[293] I have listed two passages in which "Lord" seems to be used as a human title of respect. Most Gospel passages give the impression that Lord is used as Jesus's official title, a title that cannot be separated from His person or His Divine authority. Nonetheless, we cannot be certain what the speaker intended.

[294] This is similar to the case for "Lord," in that whether the disciples intend "Master" to be a human title of respect or to mean something more is not always clear. Luke 17:13,

though, might be an example of "Master" implying faith in someone capable of Divine action.

[295] Although I have listed only five verses, most Gospel passages give the impression that "Lord" is used as Jesus's official title, a title that cannot be separated from His person or His Divine authority. Nonetheless, we cannot be certain what the speaker intended.

[296] The data in this table were determined using the indicated search criteria in Logos Software.

[297] The data in this table were determined using the indicated search criteria in Logos Software.

[298] McDowell, 34-38.

[299] Ibid., 38.

[300] We have thousands of surviving copies of portions of the New Testament coming from multiple sources and places, each of which can be compared with one another to establish the most accurate rendition of the text. As a result, copying errors and scribal clarifications are generally eliminated rather than passed along, as in the telephone game. This process of reconstructing a text as nearly as possible to its original form is called "textual criticism."

Don Stewart, "What is textual criticism? Why is the textual criticism of the Bible necessary?," *Blue Letter Bible*, accessed October 4, 2023, https://www.blueletterbible.org/Comm/stewart_don/faq/words-bible/question2-what-is-textual-criticism.cfm.

[301] McDowell, 38.

[302] Ibid., 78-79.

[303] Ibid., 79.

Acknowledgments

There are many people who have contributed to the writing of *For the Love of Truth*—completely unaware of its existence. Greg Koukl, president of *Stand to Reason*, for instance, played a major role in introducing me to thinking apologetically. I first heard him on Sunday afternoon drives between Los Angeles and San Diego, and later, as I read his books and listened to his teaching tapes. So many professional scientists and theologians added to my understanding when I pursued a master's degree with a focus on apologetics, reading book after book addressing the broad scope of the discipline. Thanks to you all.

But there are several people who deserve special thanks:

My sister, Lynn, was my first editor. From the very beginning, Lynn faithfully read and provided detailed comments on every draft of every chapter of this book. Thank you, Lynn, not only for your comments, but even more for your encouragement every step along the way!

Once the initial draft was completed and the possibility of having *For the Love of Truth* published became real, Lauren (my wife) applied her professional editing skills to polish off some of the book's "rough edges." Thank you, Sweetheart. Your revisions have made this book stronger and more accessible to many more people.

With Lauren's edits incorporated, Bonnie Lyn Smith of *Ground Truth Press* has held my hand, so to speak, leading me and *For the Love of Truth* through all the steps of the publication process. I had no idea! Thank you so much, Bonnie, for your detailed and gracious efforts in bringing *For the Love of Truth* to print.

Thanks also to those who reviewed and provided many insightful comments on the Beta Manuscript, making *For the Love of Truth* so much better: Diane G., Don T., Jeff D., Ken D., Lynn D., Matt D., Mike C., Pat C., Rich D., and Vini D-W.

About the Author

The Rev. Jack Davenport is an avid student of apologetics. Having grown up with an unquenchable desire to understand the inner workings of this world, Jack studied Engineering Physics at Lehigh University, and applied his critical thinking skills as a contractor to the U.S. Air Force and Navy in various aspects of program management for most of his career.

Tireless in his pursuit of knowledge about God and this world, Jack obtained a Master of Religious Education from Gordon-Conwell Theological Seminary and an M.A. in Science and Religion from Biola University. After retiring from the program management world, he pursued his avocation, earning a Certificate of Anglican Studies from Bethel Seminary, and was ordained a priest of the Anglican Church of North America.

For the Love of Truth is an extension of his passion to share the truth with others. He lives in the San Diego area with his wife and enjoys a round of golf and viewing the stars and planets from time to time.

Made in the USA
Middletown, DE
06 September 2024

59808686R00126